*About the author*

Kate Whiteman has been a cookery writer and editor for many years. Her numerous magazine commitments include a regular microwave column for *Taste,* and restaurant reviews for *Tatler.* In 1984 she won *The Sunday Times* Food Inspector Award. The eminent chefs Albert and Michel Roux invited her to translate and edit both their *New Classic Cuisine* and *The Roux Brothers on Patisserie,* and she was Raymond Blanc's editor on his book *Le Manoir aux Quat' Saisons. Microwave Fish Cooking* is Kate Whiteman's first book, an opportunity to share her love of cooking fish.

# ·microwave·

# FISH
## COOKING

Steam Herring Drifter

Allan Drummond.

# ·microwave·

# FISH
## COOKING

### New and Classic Recipes
### for Fish and Shellfish

KATE WHITEMAN

Macdonald Orbis

To my husband and daughters, whose healthy appetites helped me to write this book.

A Macdonald Orbis BOOK
© Macdonald & Co (Publishers) Ltd 1988
Text © Kate Whiteman 1988
First published in Great Britain in 1988
by Macdonald & Co (Publishers) Ltd
London & Sydney

A member of Maxwell Pergamon Publishing
Corporation plc

British Library Cataloguing in Publication Data

Whiteman, Kate
    Microwave fish cooking
    1. Food: Fish dishes: Dishes prepared
    using microwave ovens – Recipes
    I. Title
    641.6′92

    ISBN-356-15659-1

Typeset by Bookworm Typesetting, Manchester
Printed and bound in Great Britain by
Purnell Book Production Ltd
Member of BPCC plc

Illustrations by Alan Drummond
Drawings on pages 12-16 by Grahame Corbett

Editor: Jennifer Jones
Art Director: Linda Cole
Designer: Sheila Volpe
Photographer: James Murphy
Stylist: Sarah Wiley
Home Economist: Maxine Clark
Indexer: Myra Clark

Macdonald & Co (Publishers) Ltd
Greater London House
Hampstead Road
London NW1 7QX

ACKNOWLEDGEMENTS
The Publishers would like to thank the Panasonic Test Kitchen of Slough, Berks, for the loan of a Dimension 4 combination oven.

# CONTENTS

# FOREWORD

As a child, I spent all my holidays in the Scottish Highlands. My family were fanatical fishermen and I remember all too well interminably long days spent sitting cramped and silently in uncomfortable little boats, cold, wet and dying to go home, or tramping across windswept and sodden bogland to reach the perfect trout loch. Despite the hideous discomfort, it all seemed worthwhile when we finally tasted the wonderfully fresh fruits of those fishing expeditions; the flavour of freshly caught fish is unbeatable.

I developed a lifelong love of fish. Since those childhood days, I have rarely had the opportunity of eating fish straight from the water, but it is still one of my favourite foods. I find fresh fish fascinating to look at; even the ugly ones have a certain charm and some fish are really very beautiful.

I love the versatility of fish and shellfish and their delicate flavour. Like many people, I eat less meat than I used to and have turned more and more to fish. I never tire of it; there are so many different varieties (over 50 in Britain alone) and so many ways of cooking them. Compare that to meat, where the choice is basically between beef, lamb and pork. Fish is delicious at any meal, from breakfast to dinner; unlike meat, it makes a great starter or second course, as well as a main dish.

Microwaving brings out the very best in fish. Once you have tried fish and shellfish cooked in the microwave, you may never again want to eat traditional 'battered' fried fish. The flavour is pure, the colours remain fresh and the delicate texture is preserved. Microwaving and fish were made for each other; I have had endless enjoyment experimenting with this complementary combination and I hope that you will too.

Poisson en Croûte

# HOW TO USE THIS BOOK

The recipes are written for either metric or imperial measurements; they are approximate conversions and are not interchangeable. When measuring in teaspoons or tablespoons, these should be level; in metric measurements, 1 teaspoon = 5 ml and 1 tablespoon = 15 ml. Dishes should be cooked uncovered unless otherwise specified.

## POWER SETTINGS AND HEAT CONTROLS

All the recipes were tested in a Panasonic Dimension 4 NE 993 Combination oven with a 600W power output. Unlike conventional ovens, microwave and combination ovens are not standardized and their power settings may vary considerably. Even models with the same power output may produce different cooking results, because their performance may be affected by the size of the oven cavity and the way in which the microwaves are distributed.

---

In this book,

---

HIGH means 100% or full power output (600W)

MEDIUM means 60% or 360W power output

LOW means 30% or 180W output

DEFROST means thawing setting or 245W output

---

Unfortunately, not all microwave or combination cookers use the same terminology, so be guided by the wattage rather than by such terms as 'Medium' or 'Low' which may indicate different temperatures on different models.

However, 'High' is always equivalent to 100% or full power output. If your microwave oven has a power output of either more or less than 600W, you will need to increase or decrease the cooking times – you will have to experiment with your particular model.

If your microwave oven only has Full Power and Defrost settings, but the recipe calls for 60% power, cook on Full Power and decrease the cooking time by at least 40%. If you have a 500W oven, cook on Full Power for slightly longer than the stated time. It is essential to check the cooking constantly after half the time, otherwise you may end up with a scrambled sauce or overcooked fish.

## COMBINATION COOKING

Some recipes are best cooked in a combination oven, which combines microwave and convection heating. If you do not have one, I have given alternative instructions for microwaving or cooking conventionally. Like microwave ovens, different makes of combination ovens also use different terminology. The chart below shows the equivalent temperatures for the settings given in this book.

| Combination | Convection oven temperature | Microwave | Grill |
|:---:|:---:|:---:|:---:|
| 1 | 160C | 135W | — |
| 2 | 200C | 245W | — |
| 3 | 180C | 165W | — |
| 4 | —— | 220W | on |
| 5 | —— | 380W | on |

Above all, please remember that all cooking times are approximate. Timings can be affected by many factors, such as the temperature of the food before cooking, its shape and density and the size and dimensions of the dish and oven cavity, so it is essential to check all foods before the end of cooking. You can always add more cooking time, but can never take it away. Once food is overcooked, it is irrevocably ruined. This is especially true of fish, which can easily become tough and flavourless.

## EQUIPMENT FOR USE IN A MICROWAVE OR COMBINATION OVEN

Never use metal containers in a microwave oven, or any dish which has a metallic rim. It is not terribly wise to use your best crystal either! Most other ceramic and toughened glass containers are safe to use and of course a vast selection of specially designed microware is now available.

Dishes can be covered with a lid, a suitable plate or greaseproof paper. Recently, there have been fears that the plasticisers contained in some types of clingfilm might be hazardous to health, since they can migrate into food when heated, so only use clingfilm if the manufacturer's label states that it is suitable for use in a microwave oven.

Since combination ovens combine microwaving with conventional heat, you cannot use microware, which will melt. Use any non-metal heatproof dishes which you would use for conventional cooking. Remember that lids must also be heatproof.

At long last, fish is coming into its own. After years of being relegated to invalid food, or a poor substitute for meat on Fridays, we are beginning to appreciate the value of fish and enjoy its delicious flavour.

We have always undervalued fish, even though we are surrounded by waters full of wonderful seafood. Britain boasts over 50 different varieties of edible fish, every one a healthy food, low in fat and calories, high in protein and easily digestible – a nutritionalist's dream.

The message is finally getting through – fish is good for you, and microwaved fish is better still. Microwaving fish keeps the nutrients in the fish and the smell out of the kitchen. It produces moist, tender fish, bursting with flavour and goodness. Now that fish is back in favour and more and more varieties are appearing on the fishmonger's slab and in the supermarkets, why not be adventurous and give it a try?

Fresh fish is still often viewed with suspicion; people expect it to be expensive to buy and difficult and unpleasant to prepare. Neither is true. There is no fat and very little wastage, so that, pound for pound, it is generally no more expensive than meat. Thanks to fish farming, trout is cheap and even salmon and turbot are back in the realms of possibility.

It is really not difficult to prepare fish for cooking. Some accommodating fishmongers will do this for you and, of course, much of the fish sold in supermarkets is pre-prepared – but don't be daunted by the prospect of preparing it yourself. Just follow the instructions on pages 12–17.

As for cooking fish, you will be delighted to find how quick and easy this is in the microwave. Because the flesh is not dense, fish cooks literally in minutes and all its natural moistness and goodness is preserved. In this book, I have included a variety of recipes, from classic to exotic, which demonstrate how versatile it is. Do not give up if the specified fish is not available; substitute another type – cod for monkfish, haddock for sole – the possibilities are endless. Be bold in adapting the recipes and make the most of whatever is freshest and best. Serve fish as a simple supper or a flamboyant party dish. It will emerge from the microwave full of flavour and a treat to eat.

# CHOOSING, PREPARING AND COOKING FISH

CHAPTER 1

## HOW TO CHOOSE AND PREPARE FRESH FISH

There is no point in creating a fish dish unless the fish you use is absolutely fresh. If you are lucky enough to have a good local fishmonger, cultivate him as your friend and let him guide you as to what is freshest and best. Do not decide what fish you are going to cook until you reach the shop and can see what looks most attractive that day. If your mind is set on a particular type of fish, order it in advance to be sure that it is available when you need it.

Whole fish should have shiny, faintly slimy skin, firm flesh, bright, slightly protuberant eyes and clear red or pink gills. The tails should be firm and the scales plentiful and bright. Do not buy fish which are shedding their scales all over the counter; they have been dead too long. A good test is to push the flesh with your finger; if it feels springy, the fish is fresh. If your finger leaves a mark, the fish is stale.

Prepared fish (fillets, cutlets and steaks) should have translucent flesh and look moist and firm. All fish should have a faint, pleasant smell of the sea. If it has a strong fishy odour, do not buy it; it is not fresh. Fish which is actually bad smells unmistakably horrible.

Many books tell you that the fishmonger will be delighted to prepare your fish for you, but, alas, this is not always true. Most will gut or clean the fish, but many are reluctant to scale, skin and fillet fish to order (although they may do it if you offer to pay extra for this service), so it is as well to know how to do these things yourself.

Preparing fish is not difficult provided that you have a really sharp, flexible filleting knife. A blunt knife will mangle the delicate flesh of the fish and probably damage your fingers into the bargain, so keep your knife immaculately sharpened.

**Scaling and cleaning**: Always scale fish before cleaning. Cut off the fins and put the fish in the sink (or the scales will fly everywhere.) Hold it by

### FILLETING A ROUND FISH
1. Open out the fish and lay it on a board, cut side down. With the heel of your hand, press gently down the length of the backbone. Turn the fish over and pull out the backbone and side bones.

2. Cut the fish lengthways down the middle, trim the outside edges and lift off the two fillets.

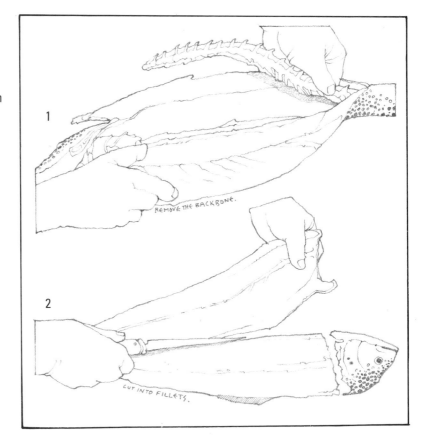

REMOVE THE BACKBONE.

CUT INTO FILLETS.

the tail using kitchen paper or a cloth to give you a better grip, and scrape off the scales with a blunt knife, working from tail to head against the lie of the scales. Do this thoroughly or loose scales may come off during cooking – and there is nothing worse than eating a mouthful of scales. Wash the fish under cold running water.

*To clean round fish*: Slit open the belly, pull out the intestines and rinse out all the blood. Rub off any final traces of blood and the black skin with a little salt and rinse again. Keep any roes and, in the case of red mullet, keep the livers, which are a great delicacy.

*To clean flat fish*: Trim off the fins, open the cavity under the gills, pull out the intestines and roe (keep the roe if you like it) and wash the fish under cold running water.

**Filleting**: Round and flat fish are filleted in slightly different ways. Round fish are divided into two fillets and flat fish are divided into four fillets.

*Filleting round fish*: The easiest way is to lay the cleaned fish on a board, cut side down. With the palm of your hand, press firmly down the whole length of the backbone. Turn the fish over and pull out the backbone and all the small side bones. Cut the fish lengthways down the middle and trim the edges of the two fillets.

*Filleting flat fish*: Flat fish are divided into four fillets, two from each side. Lay the fish on a board with the head away from you. Using a sharp filleting knife, make an incision down the backbone from head to tail. Starting with the left hand fillet, insert the knife at an oblique angle between the flesh and bone and carefully free the fillet from the bone with long, stroking movements. Turn the fish so that the head is towards you and remove the other fillet, working from tail to head. Turn the fish over and repeat the process.

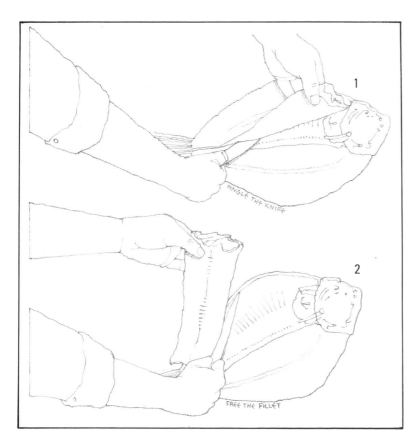

## FILLETING FLAT FISH
1. Lay the fish on a board with the tail towards you. Cut down the backbone from head to tail. Starting with the left hand fillet, insert a filleting knife at an oblique angle and carefully free the fillet from the backbone.

2. Gradually ease the fillet away, lifting it as you go. Turn the fish round so that the tail is away from you and repeat with the other fillet.

Skinning: Whole round fish can be skinned after cooking, but it is sometimes necessary to skin flat fish beforehand.

*To skin whole flat fish (e.g. sole)*: Lay the fish on a board, dark skin uppermost and with the tail towards you. Make an incision through the skin on the tail from left to right and loosen the skin on both sides.

Using a cloth, hold the tail down firmly with one hand and, with the other hand, pull the skin quickly and firmly towards the head. If you like, turn the fish over and repeat with the white skin on the other side (some people prefer to leave this white skin on).

*To skin flat fish fillets*: Lay the fillet on a board, skin side down and with the tail facing you. Make an incision through the flesh (do not cut the skin). Dip your fingers in salt to prevent them from slipping, grip the tail with one hand and, keeping the knife slightly angled away from you, work from tail to head with a sawing movement, pulling the fillet gently away from you.

Cleaning and preparing squid: Squid is usually sold frozen but, alas, unprepared, and most fishmongers are reluctant to clean it for you.

Thaw the squid if it is frozen, then rinse under cold running water. Hold the body in one hand and pull away the head gently but firmly. The soft, yellowish entrails will come out of the body; throw these away. Cut off and reserve the tentacles and remove the ink sac from the head (you can keep this to make a sauce or to tint home-made pasta).

Pull out and discard the hard, transparent quill and rinse the body inside and out under cold running water. Rub off the purplish membrane and rinse the body again. Cut off and keep the side flaps and slice the body into rings. Chop the tentacles into bite-sized pieces, or leave them whole if they are very small and you can bear the look of them.

## FROZEN FISH

If you live in the country, away from the sea, you may find it difficult to buy fresh fish, and frozen fish may be your only choice. The main problem about buying frozen fish is that you cannot apply the usual tests to ascertain whether it is fresh and of good quality – you cannot prod it, smell it or judge the brightness of its colour. Generally speaking, though, if you buy from a reputable shop with a quick turnover, you should find acceptable frozen fish.

Always buy firmly frozen packs and do not buy too much frozen fish at one time; it will only keep in the freezer for 2 to 3 months. If you are given a freshly caught fish by a generous angler, do not be tempted to freeze it yourself as the flesh will lose some of its delicate texture. Enjoy the fish while it is really fresh, or cook it and then freeze the finished dish. Most fish dishes freeze well, but do not keep them for longer than 2 months.

### SKINNING FLAT FISH
Lay the fish on a board, dark skin uppermost, with the tail towards you. Make an incision through the skin on the tail and loosen the skin on both sides. Hold the tail firmly with a cloth and firmly pull away the skin towards the head with your other hand.

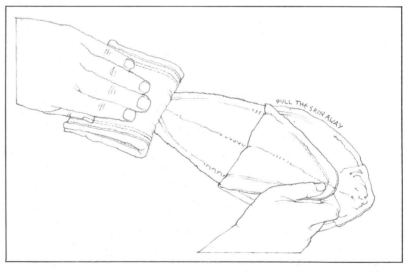

Thawing frozen fish: The microwave will thaw your fish very effectively, but take care not to over-thaw it, or it will become tough and dry. Do not wait for the fish to thaw completely; you should remove it from the microwave while it is still slightly icy.

Most frozen fish is sold as fillets, cutlets or steaks. Thaw on LOW or DEFROST for 3-4 minutes per 450 g/1 lb; remember that the thawing time will vary depending on the bulk and shape of the fish. Unless your microwave has cyclic defrost, thaw the fish in 2 minute bursts, leaving it to stand for 5 minutes after each burst. Separate the pieces as they thaw and remove each piece from the microwave as soon as it is ready.

Whole frozen fish should be thawed as above for 4-6 minutes per 450 g/1 lb. If you have a very large fish, such as a whole salmon, leave it to stand for about 10 minutes after each 2 minute burst. Rinse the cavity under cold water before cooking to ensure that the fish has thawed completely.

## BUYING FRESH SHELLFISH

It is vitally important that shellfish are bought very fresh, as they are highly perishable. They should have a fresh smell of the sea and a bright, clear colour. Live crabs and lobsters should still be lively and feel heavy for their size.

To test if a cooked lobster is fresh, pull its tail sharply; it should spring back immediately. Lobsters and crabs with missing claws are often sold cheaper and are well worth buying if you don't need the claws for presentation.

Molluscs (mussels, clams, oysters and scallops) should also feel heavy for their size. Do not buy any which have broken shells. If the shells are open, tap them sharply on a hard surface; if they do not immediately snap shut, do not buy the molluscs.

## COOKING SHELLFISH IN THE MICROWAVE

Molluscs: You will find that your microwave works wonders when it comes to opening molluscs, like mussels, small clams and cockles. Scrub the shells under cold running water to remove any barnacles, dirt or sand and, in the case of mussels, scrape off the 'beards' (which look like straggly seaweed) with a sharp knife.

Discard any which are open, or do not close quickly when you give them a sharp tap; they are dying or dead. Put the molluscs into a large casserole or bowl and cook on HIGH for 2-3 minutes per 450 g/1 lb, until they have all opened. As those on the top open, remove them and continue to cook until all the molluscs have opened. Discard any which do not.

Oysters, scallops and large clams have such thick shells that they should not be opened in the microwave. The shells absorb the microwaves and become warm, causing the molluscs to cook slightly before they open. This is both inhumane and undesirable, gastronomically speaking.

To open an oyster: Always do this yourself; if the fishmonger opens your oysters for you, the delicious liquor will drain out before you reach home. Open the oysters over a bowl to catch the liquor to use in a stock or sauce.

Wrap your hand in a tea towel and hold the oyster firmly in the palm, with the flat shell on top. Insert an oyster knife or short stubby knife into the hinge and twist to prise the shells apart. Gently free the oyster from the concave shell with a knife.

To open a scallop: Scallops are generally sold already opened and cleaned. If you do find them still in the shell, wash well (they tend to be full of sand), then place in a conventional oven, rounded side up, and heat at 150°C/300°F/Gas Mark 2 for about 10 minutes, until the shells begin to open.

Slide a fine knife blade into the gap between the shells and carefully cut the scallop away from the top shell. Rinse under cold running water, then discard the greenish-black sac and the grey beard and ease the scallop and coral away from the bottom shell. Thoroughly wash the scallop, coral and shells.

Crustaceans: It is not humane to cook live lobsters or crabs in the microwave. Either buy them ready cooked or kill them yourself. There is no very pleasant way of doing this.

Crabs: Put into a large saucepan of cold salted water (sea water is ideal, if you can get it), cover, bring to the boil and boil for 10-15 minutes. Leave to cool in the cooking water.

*To open a cooked crab*: Twist off the claws and legs. Snap the claws in half at the joint and crack them gently with the back of a heavy-bladed knife or a mallet. Pull out all the meat, scooping out the flesh from the crevices with a skewer. Scrape out any meat from the legs.

Lay the crab on its back with the tail flap towards you, put your fingers between the shell and the body and use your thumbs to push apart the upper and lower parts of the body. Remove the poisonous gills or 'dead man's fingers' (this disgusting phrase exactly describes what they look like) and press down to detach the stomach sac and mouth from the top shell. Remove all the remaining meat from the shell and discard any cartilage and pieces of shell.

**Lobsters:** Plunge a sharp, heavy knife through the cross on the back of the head; the lobster will die instantaneously. Some cooks recommend dropping lobsters into a pan of boiling water and simmering for about 10 minutes per 450 g/1 lb, but I find that this makes them tense up and the flesh becomes tough.

*To open a cooked lobster*: Twist off the claws and pincers. Gently crack the claws with a mallet and pull out the meat.

## OPENING A COOKED CRAB

1. Twist off the claws and legs and scrape out the meat from the legs.

2. Break the claws in half at the joint, crack the claws and extract the meat.

3. Lay the crab on its back, with the tail flap towards you. Push apart the upper and lower parts of the body using your thumbs.

4. Discard the greyish gills or 'dead man's fingers'.

5. Press down on the top shell to detach the stomach sac and mouth.

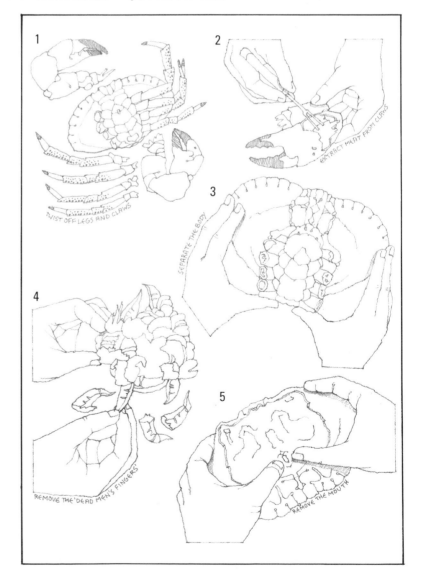

Using a sharp, heavy knife, split the lobster in half lengthways. Remove and discard the thread-like intestine, the stomach and the poisonous, spongy gills. Pull out the tail meat and bright red coral, if there is any – it is delicious.

**Prawns and scampi:** Raw prawns and scampi can be cooked in the microwave oven. Use a browning dish and cook the prawns in hot oil on HIGH for 2-4 minutes per 450 g/1 lb, stirring frequently, until they turn pink.

*To peel cooked prawns or scampi:* Hold the head between your forefinger and thumb and gently pinch and pull off the tail shell with your other hand. Pull off the head and legs. With the point of a sharp knife, remove the black thread-like intestine running down the back of the tail.

## FROZEN SHELLFISH

Obviously it is best to use fresh shellfish if you can; the flavour and texture are incomparably better than frozen. Sometimes, of course, only frozen shellfish are available. Choose only those which have no added water or 'glaze'. This detracts from the flavour and you get less shellfish and more water for your money. Your microwave will help you to thaw frozen shellfish with the minimum loss of flavour and texture.

**Frozen prawns, scampi, scallops, shrimps, cockles and mussels:** Arrange on kitchen paper (to absorb the moisture) and thaw on DEFROST for 2-3 minutes per 100 g/4 oz or 3-4 minutes per 225 g/8 oz, leaving the shellfish to stand for 5 minutes after each 2-3 minute burst. (If your oven has cyclic defrost, it will automatically switch itself on and off at intervals.) Keep separating the fish with a wooden spatula and remove them from the oven as they thaw.

**Frozen crab, lobster and crab claws:** Thaw on DEFROST for 6-8 minutes per 450 g/1 lb and leave to stand for 5 minutes after each 2-3 minute burst.

**Frozen crabmeat:** Thaw on DEFROST for 4-6 minutes per 450 g/1 lb and leave to stand for 5 minutes after each 2-3 minute burst. Keep separating the thawed meat from the block with a fork and remove it from the oven.

## TIPS FOR MICROWAVING FISH

Fish can easily become overcooked, so always microwave it for the shortest possible time, then give it a resting period to allow the delicate flesh to finish cooking by residual heat. When the fish is cooked, the flesh should be opaque and come away from the bone without any resistance. Never pierce fish with a fork to test it; you will split the delicate flesh. Insert a very fine knife blade or skewer into the thickest part, or ease the flesh away from the bone with a knife.

To ensure that fish cooks evenly, cook in a single layer in a large shallow dish. Arrange the thinner parts towards the centre of the dish or fold the tail ends of fillets underneath.

If you are cooking more than one whole fish at a time, rearrange them halfway through cooking. Pierce or slash the skin of large whole fish in two or three places to prevent it from splitting.

Always cover fish during cooking to keep in the moisture. The only exceptions to this rule are recipes for fish coated in breadcrumbs where covering would make the coating soggy. Never attempt to deep-fry fish (or anything else) in the microwave; the temperature of the oil cannot be controlled and you might start a fire.

## COOKING TIMES FOR FISH

The cooking time depends on the thickness and density of the fish, and whether it is whole or filleted. Check before the end of the given cooking time to see how the cooking is progressing; remember that the fish will continue to cook during the resting period. During this resting time, the flavour will develop fully. Fish should never be served piping hot unless it is in a soup, casserole or pie.

Whole flat fish need 3-4 minutes cooking, plus 3-4 minutes resting time per 450 g/1 lb.

Whole round fish and thick cutlets, steaks and fillets need 4-5 minutes cooking per 450 g/1 lb and 5 minutes resting, but thinner fillets will need only 3-4 minutes cooking.

Fish with denser flesh (tuna, monkfish tails, swordfish and skate wings) need 6-7 minutes cooking and 5 minutes resting per 450 g/1 lb.

These timings are only approximate; test the fish before the end of the given cooking time to check that the flesh is still succulent.

To bring out the best in fish, you need a good sauce. Because fish has such a delicate flavour, the sauce should be subtle, not overpoweringly spicy or robust. It should enhance the fish, not swamp it. The basis for many fish sauces is a good fish stock. This is extremely quick and easy to make in the microwave; keep all fish bones and trimmings and make more stock than you need, then freeze it in small yogurt pots or ice cube trays to use whenever you need it.

The sauces in this chapter are intended to accompany plainly cooked fish and shellfish. Some, like mayonnaise in its various forms, are served with cold fish; others add interest to hot dishes. Experiment with different flavourings in your sauces; you will find that a good sauce will lift the flavour of a fairly ordinary or bland fish to great heights.

# STOCKS
# AND SAUCES

CHAPTER 2

# FISH STOCK

*A good fish stock is essential for much fish cookery and is stunningly simple to make in the microwave. Whenever you buy white fish, ask the fishmonger for the heads, bones and trimmings so that you can make a good supply of stock to keep in the freezer.*

MAKES ABOUT 1 LITRE/1¾ PINTS

1 kg/2¼ lb white fish bones, heads and trimmings
1 onion, chopped
white of 1 leek or 2 leaves of bulb fennel, chopped
1 celery stalk, chopped
1 carrot, scraped and chopped
juice of ½ lemon
150 ml/5 fl oz dry white wine
6 white peppercorns
1 bouquet garni (parsley, thyme and 1 bay leaf, tied together)
1 litre/1¾ pints water

*1.* Wash the fish heads and remove the gills. Put all the ingredients into a large casserole, cover and cook on HIGH for 8-10 minutes, until boiling.
*2.* Reduce the power to MEDIUM and cook for 20 minutes. Strain through a muslin-lined sieve. For a more concentrated stock, cook the strained stock on HIGH to reduce it to the required flavour.

# COURT BOUILLON

*A poaching liquid for any kind of fish or shellfish.*

MAKES ABOUT 1 LITRE/1¾ PINTS

1 onion, quartered
2 carrots, peeled and sliced
1 small leek, sliced
1 celery stalk, sliced
1 bouquet garni (2 parsley stalks and 2 bay leaves, tied together)
2 lemon slices
300 ml/½ pint dry white wine
1 tbsp white wine vinegar
900 ml/1½ pints water

*1.* Put all the ingredients in a large casserole, cover and cook on HIGH for 8-10 minutes, until boiling. Reduce the power to MEDIUM and simmer for 20 minutes. Strain and cool before using.

# MUSTARD DILL SAUCE

*Serve this fresh, spicy sauce with any cold or raw marinated fish.*

SERVES 2-4

1 egg yolk
2 tbsp Dijon mustard
½ tsp dark soft brown sugar
1 tbsp white wine vinegar
6 tbsp sunflower oil
salt and freshly ground black pepper
1-2 tbsp chopped fresh dill

*1.* Put the egg yolk, mustard and sugar into a bowl and beat until smooth. Stir in the vinegar, then gradually beat in the oil, a little at a time, mixing it well before adding more.
*2.* When the oil is completely incorporated, season with salt and pepper, then stir in chopped dill to taste. Chill the sauce before serving.

# HERB AND YOGURT SAUCE

*The yogurt in this sauce gives it a pleasant tang which goes well with fish and scallops. Make the sauce just before you need it (it only takes a few moments), or the acid lemon juice and yogurt will discolour the herbs and turn them grey.*

SERVES 4-6

150 g/5 oz watercress
25 g/1 oz fresh parsley
2 sprigs tarragon
4 sprigs chervil
350 ml/12 fl oz Greek-style yogurt
juice of ½ lemon
2 tbsp olive oil
salt and freshly ground black pepper
a dash of Worcestershire sauce (optional)

*1.* Wash the watercress and herbs, discarding the stalks. Purée or chop very finely in a herb mill and place in a bowl.
*2.* Stir in the yogurt, lemon juice and oil and season with salt and pepper. If the sauce seems too bland, add a dash of Worcestershire sauce.
*3.* The sauce can be served warm or cold. To heat it, cover the bowl and cook on MEDIUM for 3-4 minutes, stirring halfway through. Be careful not to overheat it.

# PARSLEY SAUCE

*This classic accompaniment to white fish, such as cod or haddock, is wonderfully easy to make in the microwave. Forget the nasty lumps and dirty saucepans of yesteryear and whip up a creamy mess-free sauce in moments! Vary the sauce by substituting mushrooms or other fresh herbs for the parsley, or using 2 chopped hard-boiled eggs instead of the cream and egg yolk; the possibilities are endless.*

SERVES 4

300 ml/½ pint milk
150 ml/5 fl oz fish stock (use the poaching liquid from the fish you have cooked)
50 g/2 oz butter
3 tbsp plain flour
salt and freshly ground white pepper
6 tbsp finely chopped fresh parsley
1 egg yolk
1 tbsp double cream

*1.* Heat the milk and fish stock in a jug on HIGH for 3 minutes.
*2.* Put the butter into a large bowl (remember that milk-based sauces tend to boil over) and cook on HIGH for about 1 minute, or until melted. Stir in the flour and cook on HIGH for 30 seconds.
*3.* Strain the milk mixture into the roux, whisking continuously with a balloon whisk, then season to taste. Cook on HIGH for 3-4 minutes, whisking every minute until the sauce is smooth. Whisk thoroughly, then stir in the parsley and cook on HIGH for 2 minutes, stirring halfway through.
*4.* Whisk together the egg yolk and cream and then quickly beat them into the sauce just before serving.

# PROVENÇAL SAUCE

*A fresh-tasting sauce which adds colour and flavour to any white fish. In summer, use very ripe skinned fresh tomatoes. At other times of the year, good quality canned tomatoes have a better flavour so use those.*

### SERVES 4

1 onion, finely chopped
2 cloves garlic, finely chopped
1 tbsp olive oil
450 g/1 lb very ripe tomatoes, skinned, deseeded and chopped or a 400 g/14 oz can chopped tomatoes
1-2 tsp tomato purée
1 bay leaf
1 sprig thyme
1 tsp dark soft brown sugar
salt and freshly ground black pepper
1 tbsp chopped fresh basil (optional)

*1.* Put the onion and garlic into a large bowl with the oil, cover and cook on HIGH for 2-3 minutes, until the onion is soft.
*2.* Add the tomatoes, tomato purée, bay leaf, thyme and sugar. Cover and cook on HIGH for 5 minutes, stirring halfway through. Remove the herbs, season to taste and stir in the basil if using.

Salmon Steaks with Orange Butter Sauce (page 81)

# GOOSEBERRY SAUCE

*Gooseberry sauce, with its sharp flavour, is traditionally served with mackerel, but it is equally good with other oily fish like herrings or sardines. Use frozen gooseberries when fresh are out of season.*

### SERVES 4

450 g/1 lb green gooseberries
2 tbsp water
25 g/1 oz butter
25 g/1 oz caster or demerara sugar

*1.* Top and tail the gooseberries and place in a bowl with the water and butter. Cover and cook on HIGH for 4-5 minutes (up to 8 minutes if the gooseberries are frozen), or until the fruit is soft.
*2.* Purée the gooseberries in a blender or food processor, then rub through a sieve back into the bowl. Stir in the sugar. Cover and cook on HIGH for 1-2 minutes, or until hot.

# ORANGE OR LEMON BUTTER SAUCE

*This simple sauce is one of the very nicest to serve with fish. Use all orange or lemon, or a mixture of both.*

### SERVES 4

2 oranges or lemons
2 shallots or 1 small onion, very finely chopped
25 g/1 oz butter, chilled and diced

*1.* Grate the orange or lemon zest into a bowl and squeeze in the juice. Add the shallots and cook on HIGH for 3-5 minutes, until reduced and syrupy.
*2.* Remove the shallots, then beat the chilled butter into the sauce, one piece at a time. Cook on MEDIUM for 1 minute to heat through. Whisk and serve over or beside your chosen fish.

# HOLLANDAISE SAUCE

*This classic sauce, the perfect accompaniment to any poached fish, is incredibly easy to make in the microwave. It is best to make it in small quantities; to serve more people, just make another batch of sauce – it only takes 2 minutes!*

SERVES 2

50 g/2 oz unsalted butter
1-2 tbsp lemon juice
2 egg yolks
¼ tsp mustard powder (optional)
salt and freshly ground white pepper

*1.* Put the butter into a bowl, cover and cook on HIGH for about 1 minute, until melted. Whisk in the lemon juice, egg yolks, mustard powder, if using, and salt and pepper to taste until thoroughly blended.
*2.* Cook on MEDIUM-HIGH for 1½-2½ minutes, until thickened, stirring halfway through. If the sauce has curdled, whisk in a few drops of hot water to make it smooth. Season with a little more lemon juice if necessary and serve at once.

# SAUCE MALTAISE

Substitute the juice of 1 small blood orange for the lemon juice and stir in 1 tsp grated orange zest at the end.

# GREEN BUTTER

*This rich delicious butter goes well with any poached fish and is also delicious spread in sandwiches. Make plenty and store it in the freezer – it is always popular.*

SERVES 6

2 eggs
150 g/5 oz butter
1 tbsp olive oil
1 or 2 cloves garlic, crushed
12 spinach leaves
6 tender green lettuce leaves (not crunchy lettuce)
6 sprigs watercress
6 sprigs parsley
2 tbsp capers
½ tsp Dijon mustard
salt and freshly ground black pepper
½ tsp lemon juice

*1.* Break the eggs into a ramekin, prick the yolks twice with a cocktail stick, cover and cook on HIGH for 2 minutes. Leave to stand until the yolks are hard, then finely chop the eggs.
*2.* Cut the butter into 4 pieces, place in a bowl and cook on MEDIUM for 1-2 minutes, until softened. Place in a blender or food processor with the chopped eggs, olive oil and crushed garlic and process until smooth and creamy.
*3.* Arrange the spinach, lettuce leaves, watercress and parsley in a shallow dish, add 2 tbsp water, cover and cook on HIGH for 1-2 minutes, to blanch the leaves.
*4.* Drain well, chop roughly and add to the butter mixture along with the capers and mustard. Process until smooth, then season with salt, pepper and lemon juice. Chill until needed.

# MAYONNAISE

*A never-fail version of this versatile sauce, which so many people find difficult to make. According to your preference and the dish the mayonnaise is to accompany, use all olive oil, a mixture of olive and lighter oils or all corn or vegetable oil (grapeseed is pleasant and prevents the mayonnaise from separating in the fridge). All ingredients should be at room temperature; warm them for a few seconds in the microwave if necessary – but remember to break the eggs into a bowl first!*

SERVES 4-6

1 whole egg
1 egg yolk
1 tsp Dijon mustard
1-2 tbsp lemon juice
1 tbsp white wine vinegar
salt and freshly ground white pepper
175 ml/6 fl oz olive oil
175 ml/6 fl oz grapeseed, sunflower or corn oil

*1.* Put the whole egg and egg yolk into a blender or food processor and process for 30 seconds. Add the mustard, 1 tbsp lemon juice, vinegar and a pinch of salt and pepper and process for 30 seconds until well mixed.
*2.* With the motor running, pour in the oil in a thin, steady stream and process until it is all incorporated and the mayonnaise is thick. Taste and stir in more lemon juice if necessary.

# AÏOLI

Add 2 crushed garlic cloves to the mayonnaise (or more if you think your friends will speak to you afterwards), or add 2 peeled cloves garlic to the egg, process until smooth and continue as above.

# TARTARE SAUCE

Finely chop 1-2 teaspoons each of capers, fresh parsley, chives and tarragon, gherkins and pimento-stuffed green olives and stir them into the mayonnaise.

# ROUILLE

*This is the classic accompaniment to French fish soups. If you are feeling very brave, substitute a chopped fresh red chilli for the cayenne pepper.*

SERVES 4-6

2 eggs
4 cloves garlic, chopped
2 egg yolks
1 tsp saffron powder
1 tsp tomato purée
a large pinch of cayenne pepper or 1 fresh red chilli, chopped
100 ml/3½ fl oz olive oil
salt and freshly ground black pepper

*1.* Break the whole eggs into a ramekin and pierce the yolks 2 or 3 times with a cocktail stick. Cover and cook on HIGH for 2 minutes. Leave to stand until the yolks are hard, then separate them from the whites and discard the whites.
*2.* Crush the cooked yolks and garlic to a paste using a pestle and mortar, then place in a blender or food processor with the raw egg yolks, saffron, tomato purée and cayenne pepper or chilli.
*3.* Process for 30 seconds until smooth, then, with the motor running, pour in the olive oil in a steady trickle, until the rouille is thick and shiny. Season to taste with salt and pepper and a little more cayenne, if you like.

If I were told that I could only ever eat one kind of food again, it would be home-made soup. I love the versatility of soup; it can make a delicate and refreshing start to a meal or constitute a warming, comforting dish in its own right.

Fish soups are quick to prepare, especially if you use stock which is already boiling or very hot. Always try to make your soup with home-made fish stock. If this is not possible, use a vegetable stock cube; fish stock cubes sometimes have too concentrated a flavour.

Be adventurous when making fish soups; substitute other types of fish for those suggested and vary the flavourings to suit your own taste. Very small fish that are no use for anything else often make excellent soup. If you spend a day by the sea, why not collect tiny crustaceans from the shore and use them to concoct a delicious soup? It will take no time at all in your microwave and there is something immensely satisfying about making a dish from ingredients you have gathered yourself.

# SOUPS

CHAPTER 3

# FRENCH FISHERMAN'S SOUP

*This Burgundian soup with its bounty of fish from the local streams shows that red wine can be delicious with fish, whatever the purists say. If you are an angler, use any edible fish you happen to catch; if not, buy a selection of freshwater fish.*

SERVES 6

900 g/2 lb freshwater fish, such as pike, eel
or tench
4 carrots, peeled and sliced
2 large onions, sliced
3 cloves garlic, crushed
2 strips of orange zest
1 tbsp olive oil
bouquet garni (½ celery stalk, 1 sprig thyme,
parsley and a bay leaf tied together)
1 bottle full-bodied red wine
salt and freshly ground black pepper
50 g/2 oz butter
2 tbsp plain flour
*Garnish*
garlic croûtons (see Bouillabaisse p. 29)
chopped fresh parsley

*1.* Clean the fish and cut into bite-sized chunks. Wash the heads and tails and tie them in a piece of muslin.
*2.* Put the carrots, onions, garlic, orange zest and oil into a casserole. Cover the casserole and cook on HIGH for 10 minutes, until the vegetables are slightly softened.
*3.* Arrange the chunks of fish on the vegetables and lay the bouquet garni and bundle of fish heads on top. Pour in the wine, cover and cook on HIGH for 5 minutes, until the wine is boiling. Reduce the power to MEDIUM and cook for 10-12 minutes, until all the fish is tender.
*4.* Carefully transfer the pieces of fish to a large, warmed tureen. Discard the herbs, orange zest and bundle of heads and strain the cooking liquid into a large jug. Season to taste.
*5.* Put the butter into a large bowl and melt on HIGH for 1-2 minutes. Stir in the flour and cook for 2 minutes on HIGH to make a roux. Stir well,

then gradually stir in the strained wine to make a smooth soup.
*6.* Pour this soup over the fish and vegetables, cover the tureen and cook on HIGH for 2-3 minutes, until the soup is very hot. Garnish with the garlic croûtons, then sprinkle with chopped parsley and serve.

# CULLEN SKINK

*This rib-sticking Highland soup is just the thing for a cold winter's day. For extra internal 'central heating', add a spoonful of whisky (or more!) to each serving.*

SERVES 4

1 onion, sliced
225 g/8 oz potato, finely diced
50 g/2 oz butter
450 g/1 lb smoked haddock on the bone
600 ml/1 pint milk
freshly ground black pepper
150 ml/5 fl oz whipping cream
2 tbsp chopped fresh parsley
2 tbsp whisky (optional)

*1.* Put the onion, potato and butter into a large bowl and cook on HIGH for 5 minutes, stirring halfway through. Cut the haddock into 4 pieces and add it to the bowl. Pour in 300 ml/½ pint water, cover and cook on HIGH for 6 minutes, or until the potatoes are soft and the fish flakes easily.
*2.* Remove the haddock and flake with a fork, discarding the skin and bones. Mash the potato and onion in the cooking liquid until smooth, then stir in the milk and flaked haddock. Cover and cook on HIGH for 2-3 minutes, or until the soup is very hot. Season with pepper and stir in the cream and parsley just before serving. Add a dash of whisky to each serving if you're feeling cold or bold!

# NEW ENGLAND CLAM CHOWDER

*By all means use canned clams for this famous American dish, but make sure they are not the Italian type canned in tomato sauce, which would make the chowder horribly unauthentic.*

SERVES 4

2 potatoes, cut into 1-cm/½-in cubes
100 g/4 oz salt pork or unsmoked bacon, in one
piece, diced
15 g/½ oz butter
1 onion, chopped
2 × 200 g/7 oz cans clams
1 sprig thyme
1 bay leaf
300 ml/½ pint milk
150 ml/5 fl oz double cream
salt and freshly ground black pepper
¼ tsp cayenne pepper

*1.* Put the potatoes into a casserole with 150 ml/ 5 fl oz water, cover and cook on HIGH for 5 minutes, or until soft but not mushy. Drain and set aside.

*2.* Cut the salt pork into 5 mm/¼ in dice and lay them on a double thickness of kitchen paper, cover with another sheet of kitchen paper and cook on HIGH for 2 minutes. Leave to stand for 3 minutes.

*3.* Put the butter and onion into a large bowl, cover and cook on HIGH for 2-3 minutes, or until the onion is soft, stirring halfway through. Add the cooked potato, salt pork, the clams with their juice, the herbs, milk and cream and cook on HIGH for 3 minutes, until the soup has almost come to the boil. Stir well and microwave on MEDIUM for 4-6 minutes, until the chowder is very hot but not boiling. Remove the thyme and bay leaf, season with salt, pepper and cayenne and serve at once.

# BOUILLABAISSE

*There are those who say that it is impossible to make an authentic bouillabaisse outside the Mediterranean and to some extent they are right. Here in Britain, we certainly cannot get hold of all the fish which traditionally go into a bouillabaisse, but we can produce a pretty fair imitation using fish from our own Atlantic waters. Vary the fish according to what is fresh and available, but use at least four different kinds for an interesting flavour. Use the heads, bones and trimmings to make the fish stock.*

SERVES 6-8

2 tbsp olive oil
1 onion, chopped
2 cloves garlic, very finely chopped
white part of 1 leek, chopped
2 carrots, scraped and chopped
1 celery stalk, chopped
1 small fennel bulb, chopped
1 litre/1 ¾ pints hot Fish stock (see p. 20)
150 ml/5 fl oz dry white wine
½ tsp saffron powder ·
200 g/7 oz can chopped tomatoes
2-3 tbsp Pernod
bouquet garni (1 bay leaf, 2 parsley stalks and
1 sprig thyme, tied together)
900 g/2 lb mixed fresh fish (e.g. John Dory, conger
eel, gurnard, monkfish), cut into bite-sized chunks
450 g/1 lb cooked lobster, cut into 8 pieces or
6 cooked langoustines
2 red mullet
6 soft-shelled crabs (if you can find them)
700 g/1 ½ lb mussels, scrubbed and debearded
salt and freshly ground black pepper
Rouille or Aïoli, to serve (see p. 25)
*Garlic croûtons*
6 × 1-cm/½-in slices from a French baguette
1 clove garlic, halved
2 tbsp olive oil

*1.* First make the croûtons: rub both sides of the bread with a cut side of garlic. Put the oil in a shallow dish and heat on HIGH for 1½ minutes. Put in the bread and turn it in the hot oil. Cook on HIGH for 2 minutes, then turn the bread over and cook for another 1-2 minutes, until the croûtons are golden and crunchy. Drain on kitchen paper and set aside.

2. Put the olive oil, onion, garlic, leek, carrots, celery and fennel in the largest casserole which will fit into your microwave. Cover and cook on HIGH for 5-6 minutes until the vegetables are soft.

3. Strain the hot fish stock into the casserole containing the vegetables and add the wine, saffron, tomatoes, 2 tbsp of Pernod and the bouquet garni. Cook the mixture on HIGH for 5-7 minutes until boiling.

4. Put all the fish and crustaceans (but not the mussels) into the casserole, cover and cook on HIGH for 5-6 minutes. Remove the bouquet garni and set the bouillabaisse aside while you cook the mussels.

5. Put the prepared mussels into a large bowl, ladle in 300 ml/½ pint of the hot fish soup, cover and cook on HIGH for 5 minutes, shaking the dish occasionally and stirring halfway through. Discard any mussels which have not opened and remove the rest from their shells, leaving a few in the shell for garnishing.

6. Stir the shelled mussels and their cooking liquid into the soup, taste and season as necessary, adding a dash more Pernod if you like. Cover the casserole and heat the bouillabaisse on HIGH for 2 minutes. Serve in shallow soup plates, dividing the fish and shellfish evenly. Float a garlic croûton on the top of each serving and garnish with the reserved mussels in their shells. Serve the rouille or aioli separately.

*Left:* Rouille (page 25)
*Right:* Bouillabaisse (page 29)

# WATERCRESS AND HADDOCK SOUP

*Use some of the watercress stalks to give the soup extra flavour. Its peppery flavour contrasts well with the blandness of the haddock.*

SERVES 4

2 shallots, finely chopped
25 g/1 oz butter
2 bunches of watercress
225 g/8 oz haddock fillets
600 ml/1 pint milk
salt and freshly ground white pepper
150 ml/5 fl oz whipping cream
*Garnish*
1 tbsp whipping cream
sprigs of watercress

*1.* Put the shallots and butter into a bowl, cover and cook on HIGH for 2 minutes to soften the shallots. Set aside.
*2.* Cut off the bottom part of the watercress stalks and wash the rest under cold running water. Drain and chop coarsely.
*3.* Put the haddock and milk into a dish, cover and cook on HIGH for 3 minutes, until opaque. Skin the haddock and flake the flesh into a large bowl with the milk used for poaching. Add the shallots and chopped watercress, cover and cook on HIGH for 3 minutes.
*4.* Purée the soup in a blender or food processor until smooth. Season to taste, pour back into the bowl and stir in the cream. Cover and cook on MEDIUM for 2-3 minutes, until heated through. Spoon in a swirl of cream, garnish with sprigs of watercress and serve.

# CUCUMBER AND PRAWN SOUP

*This soup makes a perfect summer starter if served iced, but it is also excellent when hot. Be careful not to boil it when reheating, or you will spoil the delicate flavour.*

SERVES 4

25 g/1 oz butter
2 shallots, finely chopped
2 cloves garlic, crushed
1 cucumber, peeled and chopped
300 ml/½ pint milk
1 bay leaf
salt and freshly ground white pepper
225 g/8 oz cooked peeled prawns
1 tbsp chopped fresh mint
1 tsp chopped fresh dill
1 tbsp chopped fresh chives
300 ml/½ pint whipping cream
*Garnish*
2 tbsp lightly whipped cream or soured cream
4 uncooked, unpeeled prawns
sprigs of mint
fronds of dill

*1.* Put the butter, shallots and garlic into a large bowl and cook on HIGH for 2-3 minutes, or until the shallots are soft. Add the cucumber, cover and cook on HIGH for 3 minutes, or until the cucumber is tender, stirring halfway through.
*2.* Stir in the milk and bay leaf, cover and cook on MEDIUM for 5 minutes. Remove the bay leaf, pour the soup into a blender or food processor and purée until very smooth. Season to taste. Add the prawns, chopped herbs and cream and chill for at least 2 hours, or return the soup to the bowl, cover and cook on MEDIUM for 5 minutes, or until hot.
*3.* To serve, ladle the soup into individual bowls, decorate with a dollop of cream topped with an unpeeled prawn and garnish with sprigs of mint and fronds of dill.

# COCKLE SOUP

*Unless you are lucky enough to find them yourself on the beach, you will not usually be able to buy cockles still in their shells. Most fishmongers sell them already cooked and shelled. If you can track down these delicate molluscs in the shell, wash them very thoroughly and cook them like mussels (see p. 15) before making the soup. Use the strained cooking liquor instead of fish stock.*

SERVES 6

25 g/1 oz butter
50 g/2 oz streaky bacon, chopped
1 leek, finely chopped
1 celery stalk, finely chopped
4 tomatoes, peeled and chopped
1 litre/1 ¾ pints Fish stock (see p. 20)
2 potatoes, diced
450 g/1 lb cooked shelled cockles
salt and freshly ground black pepper
1 tsp lemon juice
2 eggs, beaten
*Garnish*
Garlic croûtons (see Bouillabaisse, p. 29)
chopped fresh parsley

*1.* Put the butter into a bowl with the bacon, leek, celery and tomatoes. Cook on HIGH for 3-4 minutes to soften the vegetables, then pour in the fish stock and stir well.
*2.* Add the diced potatoes, cover and cook on HIGH for 5-7 minutes, until the potatoes are tender. Stir in the cockles and season the soup with salt, pepper and lemon juice.
*3.* Pour a little of the soup on to the beaten eggs and stir the mixture back into the soup. Cook on MEDIUM for 3-5 minutes, until the cockles and soup are very hot, taking care that the soup does not boil.
*4.* Ladle the soup into warmed bowls and float a garlic croûton on the top of each. Sprinkle with parsley and serve at once.

# CRAB AND SWEETCORN SOUP

*Use either fresh, frozen or canned crab for this Chinese-style soup.*

SERVES 4

600 ml/1 pint chicken stock
2.5-cm/½-in piece of ginger root, peeled and crushed
400 g/14 oz can creamed sweetcorn
100 g/4 oz cooked white crabmeat, flaked
1 tbsp Chinese rice wine or dry sherry
1 tbsp cornflour
1-2 tsp soy sauce
1 egg white
1 spring onion, very finely chopped

*1.* Put the chicken stock and ginger into a large bowl and cook on HIGH for 3-4 minutes, until very hot. Stir in the creamed corn and heat on HIGH for 2 minutes.
*2.* Add the crabmeat. Stir the rice wine or sherry into the cornflour to make a smooth paste, then stir the paste into the hot soup. Cook on HIGH for 3-4 minutes, or until thickened. Season to taste with soy sauce.
*3.* Beat the egg white until stiff and gradually fold it into the soup. Serve in individual bowls, sprinkled with chopped spring onion.

# SMOKED OYSTER BISQUE

*This rich soup can be rustled up in moments if you have unexpected guests. If you can't find canned smoked oysters, canned mussels or clams will do, but you may need to add extra salt.*

### SERVES 4

40 g/1 ½ oz butter
2 tbsp plain flour
600 ml/1 pint milk
1 bay leaf
150 ml/5 fl oz dry white wine
freshly ground black pepper
4 × 100 g/4 oz cans smoked oysters
4 tbsp double cream
2 egg yolks, beaten
1 tbsp chopped fresh chervil
4 tsp black lumpfish roe, to garnish (optional)

*1.* Put the butter into a large bowl and melt on HIGH for 1 minute. Stir in the flour and cook on HIGH for 30 seconds to make a roux.
*2.* Heat the milk with the bay leaf on HIGH for 2 minutes, then strain it into the roux and whisk until very smooth. Cook on HIGH for 3 minutes, stirring vigorously every minute. Add the wine and season with pepper, then stir in the oysters with their juices and cook on HIGH for 3 minutes, stirring every minute.
*3.* Mix the cream and egg yolks in a bowl, pour in a little of the hot soup and whisk, then whisk the mixture back into the soup. Cook on MEDIUM for 1-2 minutes, until the soup is very hot; do not let it boil. Ladle it into individual bowls, sprinkle with chervil and top with a spoonful of lumpfish roe, if you like.

*Left:* Hot and Sour Fish Soup (page 36)
*Right:* Smoked Oyster Bisque

# HOT AND SOUR FISH SOUP

*For a really fishy flavour, make this Oriental soup with home-made fish stock, although the Chinese use chicken stock. Sea bass is the ideal fish to use, but it is fiendishly expensive, so I suggest you substitute any firm-fleshed white fish.*

SERVES 4

2 tsp dark soy sauce
2.5 cm/1 in piece of ginger root, peeled and cut into fine shreds
2 tbsp sherry vinegar
225 g/8 oz white fish fillets, skinned
900 ml/1 ½ pint hot home-made chicken or Fish stock (see p. 20)
2 tbsp Chinese rice wine or dry sherry
25 g/1 oz watercress leaves
50 g/2 oz beansprouts, cut in half
50 g/2 oz Chinese leaves, finely shredded

*1.* Mix together the soy sauce, crushed ginger and half the sherry vinegar and spread the mixture over the fish. Leave to marinate for 1 hour, turning once.
*2.* Cut the marinated fish into 1-cm/½-in dice or thin strips and place in a large bowl with the marinade. Add the stock, the rest of the vinegar and the wine or sherry, cover and cook on HIGH for 3-5 minutes, until the fish is cooked and the soup is hot.
*3.* Stir in the watercress, beansprouts and Chinese leaves and cook on HIGH for 1-2 minutes; the vegetables should still be very crisp. Serve immediately.

# CREAM OF MUSSEL SOUP

*This velvety soup is subtly flavoured with curry; if you prefer an aniseedy taste, substitute a tablespoon of Pernod for the curry powder and half a fennel bulb for the shallots.*

SERVES 6

900 g/2 lb mussels, scrubbed and debearded
275 ml/½ pint dry white wine
4 shallots, finely chopped
2 cloves garlic, finely chopped
50 g/2 oz butter
1 tbsp plain flour
225 ml/8 fl oz milk
225 ml/8 fl oz Fish stock (see p. 20)
2 or 3 pinches of curry powder
1 egg yolk
3 tbsp double cream
salt and freshly ground white pepper
1-2 tbsp finely chopped parsley, to garnish

*1.* Put the mussels and wine in a large bowl, cover and cook on HIGH for 3-5 minutes, until all the mussels have opened, shaking the bowl occasionally. Discard any closed mussels.
*2.* Strain the cooking liquor through a very fine sieve and reserve it. Take the mussels out of their shells and set aside.
*3.* Put the chopped shallots and garlic in a bowl with the butter, cover and cook on HIGH for 3 minutes, until the shallots are soft. Stir in the flour and cook on HIGH for 1 minute, then stir in the reserved cooking liquor, the milk and fish stock and flavour with curry powder to taste. Cook on HIGH for about 5 minutes, until boiling.
*4.* In a bowl, beat together the egg yolk and cream. Ladle in a little of the hot soup, stir well and pour the mixture into the remaining soup. Cook on HIGH for 2-3 minutes until the soup has thickened, but do not let it boil, or it will curdle.
*5.* Stir in the shelled mussels, reserving a few for garnish, if you like. Purée the soup in a blender or food processor until very smooth, then season to taste. If necessary, heat on HIGH for 1-2 minutes to reheat, then stir in the parsley and any whole mussels you have reserved. Serve at once.

# SCALLOP AND JERUSALEM ARTICHOKE SOUP

*The sweetness of scallops and Jerusalem artichokes combine wonderfully well in this attractive pale yellow soup, with its autumnal garnish of scallop corals and golden almonds. Buy the smoothest artichokes you can find, or forget about being thrifty and chop off all the knobbly bits before peeling!*

SERVES 6

900 g/2 lb Jerusalem artichokes
juice of ½ lemon
6 large or 12 small shelled scallops, with their corals
75 g/3 oz butter
1 onion, finely chopped
600 ml/1 pint boiling chicken stock
½ tsp saffron threads or 1 tsp saffron powder
300 ml/½ pt milk
salt and freshly ground white pepper
150 ml/5 fl oz single cream
*Garnish*
25 g/1 oz butter
3 tbsp flaked almonds
1 tbsp finely chopped fresh chervil

*1.* Peel the artichokes and immediately put them into a bowl of cold water acidulated with the lemon juice to prevent discoloration. Cut them into chunks. Slice the scallops in half vertically and prick the corals twice to prevent them from bursting during cooking.

*2.* Heat a browning dish for 5-8 minutes, or according to the manufacturer's instructions. Put in 25 g/1 oz of the butter, then the scallops and corals and cook on HIGH for 45 seconds. Turn over the scallops and corals and cook for another 30-45 seconds, until the scallops are opaque. Do not overcook them, or you will ruin the texture. Finely dice the scallops and corals and put them into separate bowls.

*3.* Put the remaining butter and the onion into a large casserole and cook on HIGH for 2-3 minutes to soften the onion slightly. Stir in the artichokes, cover and cook on HIGH for 5 minutes, stirring halfway through.

*4.* Pour in the boiling stock, saffron and milk, cover and cook on HIGH for about 5 minutes, until the liquid comes back to the boil. Reduce the power to MEDIUM and cook for 10 minutes, until the artichokes are very soft but not mushy.

*5.* Put the artichokes and liquid into a blender or food processor with half the scallops (but not the corals) and purée until very smooth. Season to taste with salt and pepper. If you want an ultra-velvety soup, rub it through a fine sieve, but this is not absolutely necessary.

*6.* Just before serving, prepare the garnish. Put the butter and almonds into a bowl and cook on HIGH for 3-4 minutes, until the almonds are golden brown, stirring frequently. Put in the diced corals and heat on HIGH for 20-30 seconds.

*7.* Stir the cream and remaining scallops into the soup, cover and reheat on HIGH for 2-3 minutes, but do not let it boil. Ladle the soup into individual bowls and scatter each serving with the corals, flaked almonds and a sprinkling of chervil. Serve at once.

Because it is light and subtly flavoured, seafood makes an ideal starter. It can be served hot or cold and sometimes, as in the case of smoked fish or oysters 'au naturel', it needs virtually no preparation.

A starter should whet your appetite for the meal that is to follow, so it should be delicate and pleasing on the eye. You will find that many of the recipes in this chapter have soft colours and textures. These make the dishes attractive to look at and to eat.

Sometimes, if you are entertaining a large number of people, it is more convenient to serve the starter with drinks before the meal instead of at the table. Small, bite-sized nibbles are ideal for this; try Coriander crabmeat balls with herb mayonnaise or Angels on horseback.

Cooking a meal should be a pleasure, not a chore, so if you are planning to serve a complicated or difficult main course, make an easy starter or a cold one which can be prepared in advance. Most of the following recipes cook in very little time, so you should be able to relax before your meal!

Many of the starters also make excellent light lunch or supper dishes. You will probably need to double the quantities and accompany the dish with a salad or some crusty bread.

# STARTERS

CHAPTER 4

# DOLMADES OF PLAICE

*Some supermarkets sell packets of vine leaves cooked in brine. These do not need pre-cooking, but rinse off the brine and pat the leaves dry before using. If you can't find vine leaves, use blanched fresh spinach or tender spring cabbage leaves instead.*

SERVES 4

225 g/8 oz plaice fillets
50 ml/2 fl oz dry white wine
100 g/4 oz cooked rice
25 g/1 oz pine nuts
3 tbsp finely chopped fresh parsley
juice and grated zest of ½ lemon
salt and freshly ground black pepper
8 prepared vine leaves
Lemon butter sauce, to serve (see p. 23)

*1.* Put the plaice into a shallow dish and pour the wine over the top. Cover and cook on HIGH for 3 minutes. Cool slightly, then strain off and reserve the cooking liquid.
*2.* Discard the skin and any bones from the plaice and flake the flesh into a bowl. Stir in the rice, pine nuts, parsley and lemon juice and zest. Season to taste with salt and pepper.
*3.* Spoon 2-3 tbsp of filling into the middle of each vine leaf and roll up. Arrange them in a shallow dish with the joins underneath and pour over the reserved cooking liquid from the fish.
*4.* Cover and cook on HIGH for 5-6 minutes, or until the vine leaves are tender. Serve with hot lemon butter sauce.

# MOULES MARINIÈRES

*For some reason, mussels are still underrated in England, perhaps because they are a bother to clean. As a result, they are wonderfully cheap – and if you can find Bouchot mussels, which contain almost no sand, they will be extremely easy to prepare. Serve this classic dish with crusty French bread and a garlicky green salad.*

SERVES 4-6

50 g/2 oz butter
4 shallots or 1 onion, finely chopped
300 ml/½ pint dry white wine
4 tbsp chopped fresh parsley
2 sprigs thyme
1 bay leaf
2.25 kg/5 lb mussels, scrubbed and debearded
2 tbsp butter
1 tbsp plain flour
freshly ground black pepper

*1.* Put the butter and shallots or onion into a large shallow dish. Cover and cook on HIGH for 3 minutes to soften the shallots. Add the wine, half the parsley, the thyme and bay leaf and cook on HIGH for 2 minutes.
*2.* Add half the scrubbed mussels, cover and cook on HIGH for 5 minutes, shaking the dish occasionally and stirring halfway through. Discard any mussels which have not opened and place the cooked mussels in a large casserole, keeping the cooking liquid in the dish. Cook the remaining mussels in the same way.
*3.* Strain the cooking liquid into a jug. Blend the butter and flour to a paste and stir it into the liquid, a little at a time. Cook on HIGH for 1-2 minutes, until slightly thickened. Season the sauce with pepper and pour it over the mussels in the casserole. Sprinkle with the remaining parsley and serve at once.

# COQUILLES ST. JACQUES

*So many inferior restaurants have ruined the good name of coquilles St. Jacques by serving scallops in a pool of greyish, floury sauce, garnished with instant mashed potato. This is a travesty of the original dish, where the creamy sauce should be the perfect partner for the crunchy scallops.*

SERVES 4

8 large shelled scallops, with their corals
50 g/2 oz butter
1 small onion, chopped
100 g/4 oz button mushrooms, thinly sliced
1 tbsp plain flour
½ tsp saffron powder
4 tbsp dry white wine
4 tbsp whipping cream
1 egg yolk, beaten
salt and freshly ground white pepper
*Topping*
25 g/1 oz butter
25 g/1 oz fine dry breadcrumbs
2 tbsp freshly grated Parmesan cheese
100 g/4 oz creamy mashed potato

*1.* Halve or quarter the scallops and pierce the corals twice with the point of a knife. Halve them, too, if they are very large.
*2.* Combine the butter and onion in a bowl, cover and cook on HIGH for 2 minutes, then add the mushrooms, stir, re-cover and cook on HIGH for 1-2 minutes, or until the mushrooms have just begun to cook.
*3.* Stir in the flour and saffron and cook on HIGH for 1 minute. Add the wine and stir until well blended. Add the scallops and corals, cover and cook on HIGH for 2-3 minutes, or until the scallops are just cooked.
*4.* Stir in the cream and egg yolk, season to taste, cover and cook on MEDIUM for 2-3 minutes, or until the sauce has thickened. Divide the mixture between 4 scallop shells or small dishes and set them aside.
*5.* To make the topping, melt the butter on HIGH for about 1 minute. Stir in the breadcrumbs and

Parmesan cheese. Sprinkle the topping evenly over the scallops and pipe a border of mashed potato around the edge.
*6.* Brown under a hot grill and serve very hot.

# ANGELS ON HORSEBACK

*Although these are traditionally served as a savoury after a meal, they make marvellous starters too. Serve each 'angel' on a circle of hot buttered toast.*

SERVES 4

8 smoked streaky bacon rashers, rinds removed
8 oysters, removed from the shell
4 large or 8 small slices of bread
butter for spreading

*1.* Stretch the bacon rashers as thinly as possible, using the flat side of a knife, and wrap one around each oyster, rolling them up tightly. Secure with wooden cocktail sticks.
*2.* Line a plate with a double thickness of kitchen paper, arrange the bacon-wrapped oysters around the edge and cover with 2 more layers of paper to prevent the bacon fat from spattering. Cook on HIGH for 3-5 minutes, until the bacon is cooked to your taste. Remember that it will continue to crisp up a little after cooking and you must not overcook the oysters.
*3.* Remove the paper and leave the 'angels' to stand while you toast the bread. Cut the toast into 8 rounds with a fluted pastry cutter and butter lavishly. Arrange the 'angels' on top and serve.

# CRAB-STUFFED MANGE-TOUT

*This attractive starter is very easy to make, if somewhat fiddly. Sit yourself at the kitchen table, listen to some lovely music and think of the end result. All the effort will seem worthwhile!*

### SERVES 6

225 g/8 oz mange-tout
a pinch of caster sugar
2 tbsp water
225 g/8 oz mixed cooked brown and white crabmeat
3 tbsp Mayonnaise (see p. 25)
a few drops of Worcestershire sauce
a pinch of paprika
salt and freshly ground white pepper
pea flowers or sprigs of flowering mint to garnish

*1.* Top and tail the mange-tout, removing any stringy bits. Put them into a shallow dish with the sugar and the water, cover and cook on HIGH for 2-3 minutes, until they are bright green and crunchy. Refresh in iced water and drain.
*2.* Mash or purée the crabmeat, depending on how smooth you want the filling to be. Stir in the mayonnaise and the Worcestershire sauce and paprika to taste and season with salt and pepper. If you chill the mixture for about 30 minutes, it will be easier to pipe.
*3.* Using a sharp knife, slit open the mange-tout along the shorter side. Put the crab mixture into a piping bag fitted with a 5 mm/¼ in nozzle and pipe it into the mange-tout. Chill before serving.
*4.* Arrange the stuffed mange-tout attractively on a serving dish and decorate with pea flowers or flowering mint if they are in season. Sweet peas make a most beautiful garnish, but don't be tempted to eat them.

*Left:* Crab-stuffed Mange-tout
*Right:* Sole and Smoked Salmon Pinwheels (page 44)

# SOLE AND SMOKED SALMON PINWHEELS

*Serve these attractive pinwheels with Herb and yogurt sauce or Sauce Maltaise. If you are feeling extravagant, use Dover sole fillets; otherwise lemon sole will do almost as well.*

SERVES 4-6

3 sole fillets, skinned
100 g/4 oz smoked salmon slices
4 tbsp Gewürztraminer or spicy white wine
½ lemon
warm Herb and yogurt sauce (see p. 21) or Sauce Maltaise (see p. 24) to serve
*Garnish*
6 lemon twists
sprigs of chervil or dill

*1.* Halve each sole fillet lengthways and neaten up the edges with a sharp knife. (Keep the trimmings to make a stock or mousse).
*2.* Cut the smoked salmon lengthways into 6 long strips, neaten the edges (eat the trimmings as chef's perks!) and lay one strip on the skinned side of each piece of sole.
*3.* Starting at the wider end, roll up each fish strip like a Swiss roll and secure with a wooden cocktail stick. Arrange the rolls around the edge of a round pie dish, with the wider ends upwards. Spoon over the wine. Cover and cook on HIGH for 3 minutes, or until the sole is just tender. Leave to stand for 5 minutes.
*4.* Carefully remove the cocktail sticks and squeeze over a little lemon juice. With a sharp, serrated knife, carefully cut each roll into 4 or 5 slices or 'pinwheels'. Arrange on serving plates, pour a little sauce at the side, decorate with a lemon twist and sprig of chervil or dill and serve at once.

# SCALLOPS WITH SAMPHIRE AND LIME

*Samphire (also known as sea asparagus) is a succulent green vegetable which grows on many beaches around Britain. Fishmongers sometimes sell this wonderful delicacy, with its aroma of the sea. If you aren't lucky enough to find samphire, substitute 3 tablespoons of chopped fresh dill or fennel fronds.*

SERVES 4-6

225 g/8 oz samphire
350 g/12 oz shelled scallops or queen scallops
juice of 2 limes
¼ cucumber, peeled, deseeded and diced
1 tbsp sunflower or grapeseed oil
freshly ground black pepper
lime triangles or twists, to garnish

*1.* Wash the samphire in several changes of cold water. Put it into a casserole with 3 tbsp water, cover and cook on HIGH for 4-6 minutes, or until just tender but still crisp, stirring every 2 minutes. Refresh in iced water, then drain.
*2.* If the scallops are large, cut them into 3 or 4 slices, leaving the corals whole. Pierce all the corals twice with a cocktail stick to prevent them from bursting and put into a dish with the scallops and lime juice.
*3.* Cover and cook on HIGH for 2-3 minutes, or until the scallops are opaque and just cooked. Leave to cool slightly, then stir in the samphire, cucumber and oil. Grind over some pepper and leave for about 1 hour for the flavours to develop.
*4.* Garnish the dish with lime triangles or twists and serve without chilling.

# POTTED SHRIMPS

*This is one of the most traditional and nicest of all starters. Try to use fresh shrimps; they are rather fiddly to peel, but their superior flavour repays all the effort. Serve the shrimps with brown bread and butter.*

SERVES 4

225 g/8 oz butter
1 blade of mace
225 g/8 oz cooked peeled shrimps
cayenne pepper
freshly grated nutmeg

*1.* Cut the butter into large cubes, reserve half for clarifying later and put the rest into a bowl with the mace. Cover and microwave on HIGH for about 2 minutes, or until melted.
*2.* Stir in the shrimps and add cayenne pepper and nutmeg to taste. Cover the bowl and cook on LOW for about 3 minutes to heat the shrimps, but do not let them boil. Remove the mace and pour the shrimps into 4 small pots or ramekins. Leave to cool while you clarify the remaining butter.
*3.* Put the butter into a clean bowl (a largish bowl will prevent spattering) and microwave on HIGH for about 2 minutes to melt. Leave for a few minutes until the milky solids settle at the bottom, then carefully spoon the clear yellow clarified butter over the potted shrimps, making sure they are completely covered.
*4.* When the clarified butter begins to set, place the pots or ramekins in the fridge and chill. Serve the chilled shrimps straight from the pots.

# SMOKED SALMON AND PRAWN PÂTÉ

*This is one of the quickest of all pâtés to prepare and the smoked salmon makes it elegant enough to grace any dinner party. Serve it with hot wholemeal rolls or toast and unsalted butter.*

SERVES 4

150 g/5 oz smoked salmon
100 g/4 oz butter
100 g/4 oz cooked peeled prawns
225 g/8 oz cream cheese
juice of 1 lemon
¼ tsp paprika
1 tbsp snipped fresh chives
salt and freshly ground black pepper
*Garnish*
4 fronds of dill
4 unpeeled prawns
8 lemon triangles

*1.* Line 4 small ramekins with clingfilm. Using scissors, cut 50 g/2 oz of the smoked salmon into julienne strips and set aside. Cut the rest into 4 slices about 10 × 7.5 cm/4 × 3 in and place a slice in the bottom of each ramekin, pressing it down gently. Keep the trimmings.
*2.* Put the butter into a bowl and melt on HIGH for 1-2 minutes. Put the prawns, half the butter and half the cream cheese into a blender or food processor and blend until smooth. Add lemon juice and paprika to taste.
*3.* Divide the mixture between the ramekins and firm it down with the back of a spoon.
*4.* Put the smoked salmon trimmings, the rest of the butter and cream cheese and the chives into the blender or food processor and process until smooth. Season to taste with salt and pepper.
*5.* Arrange the julienne of smoked salmon over the prawn pâté, then divide the smoked salmon pâté between the ramekins. Smooth over the surface, cover and chill.
*6.* To serve, invert the ramekins on to small plates and carefully peel off the clingfilm. Top each with a frond of dill and a prawn and place 2 lemon triangles at the side.

# MOUSSELINES OF PINK TROUT WITH TARRAGON SAUCE

*These light mousselines are equally delicious made with salmon. Not everyone likes tarragon; if you are among their number, make the sauce with watercress instead. Use a really full-flavoured fish stock for this recipe.*

SERVES 4

225 g/8 oz pink trout fillets, skinned
1 egg
2 tbsp concentrated Fish stock (see p. 20)
50 g/2 oz cream cheese
salt and freshly ground white pepper
1-2 tsp lemon juice
1 tbsp finely chopped fresh tarragon or dill (optional)
4 sprigs tarragon or dill
butter, for greasing
sprigs of tarragon, to garnish
*Sauce*
1 tbsp butter
1 shallot, finely chopped
3 tbsp chopped fresh tarragon or 25 g/1 oz watercress leaves, finely chopped
150 ml/5 fl oz concentrated Fish stock (see p. 20)
100 ml/3 ½ fl oz whipping cream

*1.* Cut the trout into chunks and purée in a blender or food processor with the egg, 2 tbsp fish stock and cream cheese until smooth. Season to taste with salt, pepper and lemon juice.
*2.* Rub the mixture through a fine metal sieve so that it is really smooth and creamy, then stir in the chopped tarragon or dill if using. Lay sprigs of tarragon or dill around the sides of 4 greased ramekins or cups and spoon in the trout mixture. Cover and cook on LOW for 5-7 minutes, until the mousselines are just set. Leave to stand while you make the sauce.
*3.* Put the butter and the chopped shallot into a 600 ml/1 pint bowl and cook on HIGH for 2-3 minutes, or until the shallot is soft. Stir in the chopped tarragon or watercress, fish stock and

cream and cook on HIGH for 2 minutes, until the sauce is slightly reduced, then rub through a sieve.
*4.* Run a knife blade round the edge of the ramekins or cups and unmould the mousselines on to warmed plates. Spoon a little sauce over the top and around the edge and serve immediately, garnished with a sprig of tarragon.

# ROLLMOPS

*Serve these savoury soused herrings with a salad of cucumber in dill-flavoured soured cream.*

SERVES 4

4 herrings, filleted
salt
100 ml/3 ½ fl oz white wine vinegar
100 ml/3 ½ fl oz water
4 black peppercorns
1 tsp whole pickling spice
1 onion, sliced into thin rings
fronds of dill, to garnish

*1.* Season the herring fillets with salt. Starting from the tail end, roll them up, skin side out, and secure with wooden cocktail sticks. Lay them in a shallow dish and add the vinegar, water, peppercorns and pickling spice. Scatter the onion rings over the top.
*2.* Cover and cook on HIGH for 6-8 minutes, rotating the dish halfway through cooking. Leave the rollmops to cool in the cooking liquid, then chill until ready to serve.
*3.* Drain the rollmops then top each one with an onion ring from the marinade and decorate with fronds of dill before serving.

Mousselines of Pink Trout with Tarragon Sauce

# POTTED CRAB

*This old English recipe was used to preserve shellfish in the days before refrigeration. It is delicious made with fresh crab, but frozen crabmeat is fine too. Serve the potted crab with brown bread and butter.*

SERVES 6

450 g/1 lb mixed white and brown cooked crabmeat
50 g/2 oz butter
200 ml/7 fl oz double cream
50 ml/2 fl oz medium sherry or dry Madeira
a dash of Worcestershire sauce
salt and freshly ground black pepper
50 g/2 oz clarified butter, to seal (see Potted shrimps p. 45)
lemon wedges, to garnish

*1.* Mix together the white and brown crabmeat. Put the butter into a bowl and cook on HIGH for 1 minute to melt it. Stir in the mixed crabmeat, cover and cook on MEDIUM for 5 minutes, or until thoroughly heated, stirring every minute.
*2.* Add the cream, stir well, then cover and cook on MEDIUM for 5 minutes, until the mixture is very thick. Purée in a blender or food processor until smooth, then stir in the sherry or Madeira and season to taste with Worcestershire sauce, salt and pepper.
*3.* Spoon the crab mixture into 6 ramekins, cool and seal with a film of clarified butter. Chill, then serve garnished with lemon wedges.

# CREAMY SALMON MOUSSE WITH PRAWNS

*Serve small portions of this delectable mousse on a bed of thinly sliced cucumber. It really is one of the nicest of all summer starters.*

SERVES 6

450 g/1 lb salmon fillet
50 ml/2 fl oz Fish stock (see p. 20)
1 tbsp powdered gelatine
freshly grated nutmeg
¼ tsp mustard powder
1 tsp lemon juice
a large pinch of cayenne pepper
3 tbsp double cream
salt and freshly ground white pepper
2 egg whites
*Garnish*
12 cooked unpeeled prawns
fronds of dill

*1.* Put the salmon into a dish with the fish stock, cover and cook on HIGH for 4 minutes. Leave to cool, then discard the skin and any bones and strain the cooking stock into a small bowl.
*2.* Stir the gelatine into the strained stock and cook on HIGH for 30-40 seconds to dissolve the gelatine.
*3.* Put the salmon in a blender or food processor with the dissolved gelatine, nutmeg and mustard to taste, the lemon juice, cayenne pepper and cream and process until smooth. Season to taste with salt and pepper. Transfer to a large bowl and chill until the mixture is almost set.
*4.* Beat the egg whites with a pinch of salt until stiff (if they have come straight from the fridge, heat them on HIGH for about 20 seconds to bring them to room temperature). Fold them into the mousse mixture, place in a serving dish and chill until completely set.
*5.* Decorate the top of the mousse with prawns and fronds of dill before serving.

# SCALLOPS À LA MAGLOIRE

*This rich dish combines the sea fresh flavours of scallops, mussels and prawns with the peaty scent of malt whisky. If you prefer, substitute brandy or Pernod for the whisky.*

SERVES 8

8 small scallops with their shells
100 ml/3 ½ fl oz dry white wine
4 tbsp malt whisky (a good peaty one, like Laphroig)
1 tbsp lemon juice
2 sprigs fresh tarragon or ½ tsp dried tarragon
2 shallots or 1 small onion, finely chopped
900 g/2 lb mussels, scrubbed and debearded
50 g/2 oz cooked peeled prawns
25 g/1 oz butter
25 g/1 oz plain flour
2 tbsp double cream
salt and freshly ground white pepper
2 tbsp fine fresh white breadcrumbs
2 tbsp grated Gruyère cheese
a pinch of cayenne pepper

*1.* Remove the scallops from their shells and wash both scallops and shells. If there are any corals, pierce them twice with the point of a knife to prevent them from bursting during cooking.
*2.* Put the shelled scallops and corals into a dish with half the wine, half the whisky, the lemon juice, tarragon and shallots or onion. Cover and cook on HIGH for 2-3 minutes, until the scallops are just opaque. Set aside.
*3.* Put the mussels into a large bowl with the rest of the wine and cook on HIGH for 3-5 minutes, until all the mussels have opened, shaking the bowl from time to time and stirring halfway through. Discard any mussels which have not opened.
*4.* Reserve a few mussels in the shell for garnish and shell the rest. Strain the cooking liquor from the scallops and mussels into a jug. Put the scallops and corals back into the washed shells, divide the shelled mussels between the scallop shells and arrange the prawns on top.

*5.* Put the butter into a bowl and melt on HIGH for 30-40 seconds. Stir in the flour to make a smooth roux, then gradually pour on the scallop and mussel liquor, stirring continuously, until the sauce is smooth. Cook on HIGH for 2-3 minutes, until boiling, then stir well. Stir in the cream and the rest of the whisky and season to taste with salt and pepper. Cook on MEDIUM for 2-3 minutes, until the sauce is thick and velvety.
*6.* Spoon the sauce over the scallops, mussels and prawns and sprinkle the breadcrumbs, cheese and cayenne pepper on top. Brown quickly under a hot grill, surround each scallop shell with some of the reserved mussels and serve at once.

# SMOKED TROUT COCOTTES

*Serve this quick and tasty hot starter with crusty French bread.*

SERVES 4

2 tsp butter
225 g/8 oz smoked trout fillets
4 tomatoes, skinned, deseeded and diced
4 tbsp double cream
1 ½ tbsp freshly grated Parmesan cheese

*1.* Butter 4 ramekins. Flake the trout flesh, mix it with the diced tomato and divide the mixture between the ramekins.
*2.* Pour a spoonful of cream over each one and top with Parmesan cheese.
*3.* Put on a high rack and cook on COMBINATION 5 for 5-7 minutes, until browned or microwave on HIGH for 2-3 minutes until heated through, then brown under a preheated grill.

OVERLEAF
*Left:* Oyster Rockefeller (page 52)
*Right:* Scallops à la Magloire

# OYSTERS ROCKEFELLER

*There are those who believe that oysters should never be cooked, but eaten raw with just a squeeze of lemon. Others (myself included) find the texture of raw oysters unpalatable, though the flavour is exquisite; this classic American recipe cooks these delicate shellfish to perfection without affecting their delicacy. Traditionally, the oysters are sprinkled with absinthe (Pernod is more legal and less lethal) before cooking.*

SERVES 1-2

4 live Colchester or Whitstable oysters
100 g/4 oz fresh spinach
2 tbsp double cream
salt and freshly ground black pepper
a few drops of Pernod (optional)
4 tsp finely chopped fresh parsley
juice of ½ lemon
a few drops of Worcestershire sauce
1 rasher of streaky bacon

*1.* Hold the oysters in a tea towel, flat side up. Insert a blunt knife into the hinge and open the oysters over a bowl lined with a fine sieve to catch the juices. Slide the oysters out of the shells and reserve the concave shells.
*2.* Wash the spinach in several changes of cold water, remove the stalks and put the leaves into a bowl. Cover and cook on HIGH for 1 minute. Squeeze gently with your hands to remove excess water. Finely chop the cooked spinach, stir in the cream and oyster juices and season to taste.
*3.* Divide the spinach between the oyster shells and lay an oyster in each shell. Sprinkle over a drop or two of Pernod if you like. Top with chopped parsley and add a few drops of lemon juice and Worcestershire sauce. Season to taste with salt and pepper.
*4.* Trim off the rind and fat from the bacon. Place the rasher on a double thickness of kitchen paper and cook on HIGH for 45-60 seconds, until cooked.
*5.* Cut the rasher into 4 squares and place a square over each oyster. Arrange the shells in a dish and cook on HIGH for 2 minutes – the oysters should be barely cooked. Serve immediately.

# SMOKED HADDOCK PÂTÉ

*This pâté can be as smooth or as chunky as you like; I prefer mine rather coarse, but if you like a creamy texture, just purée it for longer. For a less calorific starter, substitute cottage or curd cheese for the cream cheese. Serve with crusty wholemeal French bread.*

SERVES 4-6

450 g/1 lb smoked haddock fillets or, better still,
700 g/1½ lb finnan haddie on the bone
300 ml/½ pint milk
100 g/4 oz low fat cream cheese
4 sprigs parsley
cayenne pepper
lemon juice
fresh parsley, to garnish

*1.* Put the haddock into a dish and pour over the milk. Cover and cook on HIGH for 5-6 minutes, until the flesh flakes easily with a fork. Leave to cool in the cooking liquid.
*2.* Skin the cooled fish and remove the bones if you are using finnan haddie. Flake the fish into a blender or food processor, add the cooking liquid, cream cheese, parsley, a pinch of cayenne pepper and lemon juice to taste.
*3.* Process until the pâté is the texture you like, then transfer it to a serving bowl or individual ramekins, cover and chill. Sprinkle the top of the pâté with a little cayenne pepper, and garnish with parsley to serve.

# CHILLI PRAWNS

*A spicy dish to start off your dinner party with a zing! It also makes an excellent main course served on a bed of saffron rice. Only use fresh cooked prawns for this recipe; their flavour and texture is incomparably better than frozen.*

SERVES 6

50 ml/2 fl oz olive oil
1 small onion, finely chopped
1 clove garlic, finely chopped
1 fresh red chilli pepper, deseeded and finely chopped, or a large pinch of dried red chilli pepper flakes
3 tbsp finely chopped fresh parsley
400 g/14 oz can chopped tomatoes
1 tsp lemon juice
salt and cayenne pepper
700 g/1 ½ lb cooked peeled prawns

*1.* Put the oil and onion into a bowl and cook on HIGH for 3-4 minutes, until the onion is soft.
*2.* Stir in the garlic and red chilli or chilli flakes and cook on HIGH for 1 minute to blend the flavours. Add the parsley and tomatoes with their juice and season with lemon juice, salt and cayenne pepper to taste. Cook on HIGH for 5-8 minutes, until the sauce has thickened.
*3.* Add the prawns, stir well, cover and cook on HIGH for 2-3 minutes, until the prawns are very hot. Serve at once.

# CORIANDER CRABMEAT BALLS WITH HERB MAYONNAISE

*When entertaining a large number of guests, it is sometimes easier to serve a starter with drinks before going to the table for the main course. These aromatic crabmeat balls, served with an unusual fresh-tasting mayonnaise dip, are perfect for such an occasion.*

SERVES 6

450 g/1 lb mixed cooked brown and white crabmeat
2 egg yolks
25 g/1 oz fresh breadcrumbs
3 spring onions, finely chopped
1 tbsp capers, drained and chopped
grated zest and juice of 1 lemon
1 tsp garam masala powder or ½ tsp ground cumin and ½ tsp ground coriander
a pinch of cayenne pepper
4 tbsp finely chopped fresh coriander
*Herb mayonnaise*
300 ml/½ pint Mayonnaise (see p. 25)
150 ml/5 fl oz crème fraîche or Greek-style yogurt
finely grated zest of 1 lemon
1 tbsp snipped fresh chives
1 tbsp finely chopped fresh mint

*1.* Mix together all the crabmeat ball ingredients, except the fresh coriander, and shape into 24 small balls.
*2.* Arrange half the balls round the edge of a plate and cook on HIGH for 2-3 minutes, or until just firm. Cook the remaining balls in the same way. Roll them all in the chopped coriander.
*3.* Mix together all the mayonnaise ingredients and serve as a dip.

# SHRIMP-STUFFED AVOCADOS

*A warm variation on the ever-popular theme of avocado with prawns.*

### SERVES 4

2 ripe avocados
juice of ½ lemon
½ small onion or 2 spring onions, very finely
chopped
100 g/4 oz cooked peeled shrimps
150 ml/5 fl oz sour cream
2 or 3 drops of Tabasco sauce
2 tbsp chopped fresh chervil
salt and freshly ground black pepper
a pinch of cayenne pepper

*1.* Halve and stone the avocados and scoop out the flesh into a bowl. Dice the flesh and mix immediately with the lemon juice.

*2.* Stir in all the other ingredients, except the cayenne pepper, seasoning to taste with salt and pepper. Pile the mixture back into the avocado shells and cook on MEDIUM for 2-3 minutes, until warm. Sprinkle with a little cayenne pepper and serve at once.

*Left:* Coriander Crabmeat Balls with Herb Mayonnaise (page 53)
*Right:* Shrimp-stuffed Avocados

# CODDLED EGGS WITH SMOKED SALMON

*This ever-popular starter takes only moments in the microwave. Serve the eggs with fingers of buttered toast and let your guests dip them into the soft egg yolks. Top with a spoonful of salmon eggs for a touch of glamour.*

SERVES 4

100 g/4 oz smoked salmon
4 large eggs
2 tsp snipped fresh chives
2 tbsp whipping cream
freshly ground black pepper
4 tsp salmon eggs (optional)

*1.* Cut the smoked salmon into fine strips and divide it between 4 ramekins. Break an egg into each and prick the yolks twice with a cocktail stick to prevent them from bursting during cooking.
*2.* Mix the chives into the cream and spoon over the eggs. Cover the ramekins and cook on MEDIUM for 4 minutes.
*3.* Leave to stand for 2 minutes, then grind over a little pepper. Top with a spoonful of salmon eggs, if using, and serve.

# FIELD MUSHROOMS STUFFED WITH CRAB

*Most supermarkets now sell large open field mushrooms, although, of course, if you can find them growing wild, they will be doubly delicious. Two of these make a good lunch dish, served with hot garlic bread and a salad.*

SERVES 4

4 large open field mushrooms, about 100 g/4 oz each
1 tbsp sesame oil
4 spring onions, finely chopped
1 tbsp butter
100 g/4 oz cooked white crabmeat
4 tbsp fresh brown breadcrumbs
1 egg, lightly beaten
2 tbsp double cream
2 tbsp chopped fresh parsley
2.5 cm/1 in piece of ginger root, peeled, or ¼ tsp ground ginger
75 g/3 oz shelled cashew nuts, coarsely chopped
salt and freshly ground black pepper

*1.* Remove the mushroom stalks and smear the outside of the caps with the oil. (Keep the stalks to use for soups or sauces.)
*2.* Put the spring onions and butter into a large bowl and cook on HIGH for 2-3 minutes, until the onions are soft. Stir in the crabmeat, breadcrumbs, egg, cream and parsley and mix well. Crush the ginger root in a garlic press to extract the juice and stir in the juice or ground ginger, then the chopped cashew nuts. Season to taste with salt and pepper.
*3.* Pile the mixture into the mushroom caps and arrange in a shallow dish large enough to hold them all in one layer. Cook on COMBINATION 5 for about 8 minutes, until the mushrooms are tender and the filling is crisp, or microwave on HIGH for 6-8 minutes, then brown under a hot grill.

# KIPPER PÂTÉ

*This is one recipe where boil-in-the-bag kipper fillets really come into their own. Chill the pâté slightly and serve it with hot wholemeal toast.*

### SERVES 6

2 × 225 g/8 oz packets of frozen boil-in-the-bag
kipper fillets
175 g/6 oz butter
juice of ½ lemon
a pinch of cayenne pepper
lemon twist and parsley sprig, to garnish

*1.* Pierce the bags containing the kipper fillets with the point of a knife and cook on HIGH for 5-7 minutes. Leave to cool slightly, then take the kippers out of the bags, reserving the cooking juices, and remove the skin.
*2.* Put the butter into a bowl, cover and cook on MEDIUM until softened. If you like a coarse-textured pâté, mash the kippers with the softened butter and the reserved cooking juices. Add lemon juice and cayenne pepper to taste. For a smooth pâté, purée the ingredients in a blender or food processor.
*3.* Pile the pâté into a serving dish, cover and chill. Decorate with a lemon twist and parsley sprig just before serving.

# FLORIDA CRAB WITH PINK GRAPEFRUIT

*This imaginative combination of flavours marries surprisingly well to make a most refreshing starter. Try to use pink grapefruit if possible; they have a sweeter, more delicate flavour and look ravishingly pretty when you dig down beneath the crab topping. If you can find fresh coconut (infinitely nicer than dried), stir some of the water into the crab mixture for extra flavour.*

### SERVES 4

2 pink grapefruit
1 onion, finely chopped
2 cloves garlic, finely chopped
1 small red or green pepper, cored, deseeded and
finely chopped
1 tbsp palm or groundnut oil
2 tomatoes, peeled, deseeded and finely diced
50 g/2 oz pine nuts
½ fresh coconut, grated or 2 tbsp desiccated
coconut
225 g/8 oz white crabmeat, preferably fresh
salt
a large pinch of cayenne pepper

*1.* Halve the grapefruit and, using a serrated knife, loosen the segments. Discard the pips and centre cores.
*2.* In a bowl, combine the onion, garlic, pepper and oil and cook on HIGH for 3 minutes, until soft.
*3.* Stir in the tomatoes, pine nuts, coconut and crab and season with salt and cayenne pepper to taste. If you have fresh coconut water, stir in enough to make the mixture moist but not sloppy.
*4.* Divide the crab mixture between the grapefruit, piling it up in the centre. Place the filled grapefruit in a dish and heat on HIGH for 2-3 minutes until warm. Serve at once, or leave to cool and serve chilled.

# Substantial Starters and Light Lunches

These dishes are perfect for an elegant lunch, brunch or supper when you do not want a heavy meal. Most can be prepared in advance so that you do not have to engage in frantic preparation for what should be a relaxing occasion.

All these recipes can be served in smaller quantities as starters or even as a fish course between the hors d'oeuvre and main course. This idea of a small second course is becoming fashionable again; serve tiny helpings as an appetizing prelude to the main dish.

## STRIPED FISH TERRINE

*Any firm white fish is suitable for this terrine, which can be served cold or just warm with Hollandaise sauce (see p. 24).*

### SERVES 8

450 g/1 lb salmon fillet, skinned
450 g/1 lb sole fillets, skinned
3 egg whites
salt and freshly ground white pepper
6 tbsp double cream
75 g/3 oz frozen spinach, thawed and finely chopped
freshly grated nutmeg
1 tbsp finely snipped fresh chives
lemon juice
fresh chives, to garnish

*1.* Line a terrine approximately 20 × 8 cm/8 × 3¾ in with microwave-safe clingfilm. Slice the salmon fillet horizontally as thinly as possible, then cut it and the sole fillets into long slices, about 2.5 cm/1 in wide.
*2.* Arrange alternate slices of salmon and sole fillet to line the terrine, reserving enough slices to cover the top. You should be left with about

225 g/8 oz sole and 100 g/4 oz salmon.
*3.* Beat the egg whites with a pinch of salt until well risen but not stiff. Finely purée the remaining sole in a blender or food processor, season lightly and fold in two-thirds of the egg whites, then 4 tbsp cream. Halve the mixture, stir the spinach into one half and season with a pinch of nutmeg. Fold the snipped chives into the other half of the mixture.
*4.* Purée the remaining salmon in the blender or food processor, add a dash of lemon juice, then fold in the remaining egg whites and cream.
*5.* Spread the spinach mixture in the terrine and smooth the surface with a spatula. Make another layer of salmon mixture, then one of white sole mixture. Cover with the reserved fish fillet slices, then with microwave-safe clingfilm. Cook on HIGH for 5-7 minutes. The top fillets will still look slightly opaque. Leave to stand for 5 minutes.
*6.* Remove the clingfilm and lay a wire rack over the top of the terrine. Invert the rack and terrine on to a baking tray to catch the liquid which will drain out of the terrine. Keep the liquid to make a fish stock.
*7.* Leave for about 10 minutes, turn the terrine over again, then invert it on to a serving dish. Using a serrated knife, carefully cut into slices to reveal the pretty layers, or chill the terrine until ready to serve.

Striped Fish Terrine

# CREAMED FISH VOL-AU-VENT

*Smoked fish also makes a delicious filling for vol-au-vent; smoked trout is particularly good. If you haven't got a combination oven, bake the vol-au-vent cases in a conventional oven and fill them with the fish mixture at the last moment so that they remain light and crisp.*

SERVES 4

450 g/1 lb cod or haddock fillets
100 ml/3 ½ fl oz dry white wine
1 bay leaf
4 parsley stalks
40 g/1 ½ oz butter
25 g/1 oz plain flour
225 ml/8 fl oz milk
salt and freshly ground black pepper
lemon juice
1 egg yolk
2 tbsp whipping cream
100 g/4 oz cooked peeled prawns
1 tsp chopped fresh tarragon
4 large or 8 medium baked vol-au-vent cases

*1.* Put the fish into a shallow dish with the wine, bay leaf and parsley stalks. Cover and microwave on HIGH for 4-5 minutes, until just cooked. Strain off and reserve the cooking liquid. When the fish is cool enough to handle, discard the skin and any bones and flake the flesh.

*2.* Put the butter into a bowl and microwave on HIGH for 45 seconds, until melted. Stir in the flour and cook on HIGH for 1 minute. Using a balloon whisk, whisk in the strained fish cooking liquor, then the milk and cook on HIGH for 3 minutes, until the sauce has thickened, stirring every minute to keep it smooth. Season to taste with salt, pepper and lemon juice.

*3.* In a small bowl, beat together the egg yolk and cream. Ladle in a little of the hot sauce, stir well, then pour the mixture back into the sauce. Cook on MEDIUM for 1-2 minutes, stirring halfway through. The sauce should be thick and shiny. Stir in the flaked fish, prawns and tarragon and set aside.

*4.* Arrange the vol-au-vent cases on a baking tray and heat on COMBINATION 2 for 5-10 minutes, until hot and golden. Alternatively, preheat a conventional oven to 230°C/450°F/Gas Mark 8 and heat the vol-au-vent cases for about 6 minutes until very crisp. If necessary, reheat the fish mixture on MEDIUM for 2-3 minutes (but do not let it boil), then spoon it into the vol-au-vent cases. Serve at once, or the pastry will go soggy.

# CHILLED PILAFF RING

*This decorative spiced pilaff makes an interesting lunch or buffet dish. It looks particularly attractive with a mound of cornsalad and curly endive piled into the centre. You can use any kind of fish or shellfish; smoked oysters or mussels make an interesting addition.*

SERVES 6

350 g/12 oz long grain rice
a large pinch of saffron threads
salt
600 ml/1 pint boiling water
2 tbsp sunflower oil
1 tbsp curry powder
50 g/2 oz pine nuts
1 clove garlic, crushed
1 small red pepper, cored, deseeded and very finely diced
4 spring onions, finely chopped
cayenne pepper
100 g/4 oz can smoked oysters, drained (optional)
50 g/2 oz sultanas
225 g/8 oz cooked peeled prawns
3 tbsp chopped fresh coriander or parsley
*Dressing*
4 tbsp olive oil
2 tbsp red wine vinegar
4 tbsp natural yogurt
2 tbsp chopped fresh coriander

*1.* Put the rice into a large bowl with the saffron and 1 tsp salt and pour over the boiling water. Cover and cook on HIGH for 10-12 minutes, until the rice is just tender and the liquid has been absorbed. Leave to stand while you make the dressing.

*2.* Whisk together all the ingredients for the dressing until thoroughly blended. Stir the dressing into the hot rice.

*3.* Put the sunflower oil, curry powder, pine nuts, garlic, diced pepper and spring onions into a shallow dish and cook on HIGH for 2 minutes, until the pepper is slightly softened. Stir into the rice, season to taste with salt and cayenne pepper and leave until cold.

*4.* Halve the smoked oysters, if using, and stir into the cold rice, together with the sultanas, prawns and coriander. Lightly oil a 1.4 litre/2 ½ pint ring mould and spoon in the rice mixture, pressing it down firmly. Chill until needed.

*5.* To serve, invert the rice ring on to a serving dish and fill with green salad or serve the salad separately.

# SMOKED SALMON AND SPINACH ROULADE

*This versatile roulade can be filled with all manner of fishy delights, like smoked haddock, shellfish or taramasalata. It can also be served hot, rolled around a mixture of smoked salmon and soft garlic and herb cheese, softened with a little cream. Serve it with a crisp green salad.*

SERVES 4-6

sunflower oil, for greasing
450 g/1 lb fresh spinach or 175 g/6 oz frozen chopped spinach
15 g/½ oz butter
4 eggs, separated
freshly grated nutmeg
1 tsp grated lemon zest
salt and freshly ground black pepper
*Filling*
150 g/5 oz cream cheese (low fat, if you prefer)
150 ml/5 fl oz soured cream
100 g/4 oz smoked salmon
2 tsp chopped fresh dill or chives
fresh chives, to garnish

*1.* Preheat a convection oven to 170°C/325°F or a conventional oven to 190°C/375°F/Gas Mark 5.

*2.* Grease a 33 × 23 cm/13 × 9 in Swiss roll tin and line it with greaseproof paper or baking parchment.

*3.* Wash the fresh spinach, shake dry and discard the stalks. Put the leaves in a dish, cover and cook on HIGH for 3-4 minutes until tender, stirring halfway through. If using frozen spinach, defrost it in the microwave for about 10 minutes. Drain the spinach very thoroughly and gently squeeze out the excess moisture with your hands.

*4.* Briefly purée the spinach in a blender or food processor with the butter; the texture should not be too smooth. Beat the egg yolks until creamy, then beat in the spinach, nutmeg to taste and the lemon zest. Season with salt and pepper.

*5.* Heat the egg whites in the microwave on HIGH for 20-30 seconds; this will increase the volume when they are beaten. Beat them with a pinch of salt until firm but not too dry, then fold them

lightly but thoroughly into the spinach mixture with a metal spoon. Spread the mixture in the prepared tin, smoothing it evenly with a spatula. Bake in the preheated convection or conventional oven for 10-12 minutes, until firm but still springy to the touch.

6. Meanwhile, prepare the filling. Soften the cream cheese in the microwave on MEDIUM for about 30 seconds, then mix in the soured cream. Cut the smoked salmon into thin strips; if you have any to spare, put a few strips aside for garnish. Carefully fold into the cream mixture. Stir in the dill or chives and season to taste. Chill the salmon in the fridge until needed.

7. Remove the roulade from the oven and invert it on to a sheet of baking parchment. Lay a damp tea towel over the lining paper and leave to cool for 1 hour or refrigerate overnight. Remove the tea towel and carefully peel off the paper.

8. Spread the filling smoothly and evenly over the roulade and roll up like a Swiss roll. Chill until ready to serve.

9. To serve, carefully cut the roulade into 2.5 cm/ 1 in slices, using a serrated knife. Use a fish slice to transfer the slices to the serving platter. Garnish with strips of salmon, if using, and fresh chives. It is not advisable to let your guests help themselves, as they may make a terrible mess and spoil the pretty green and pink whirls of the roulade!

Smoked Salmon and Spinach Roulade (page 61)

# SPRINGTIME TERRINE

*I have called this light terrine of lemon sole 'Springtime' because of its fresh colours – the bright greens and pastel pinks of spring – but it is delicious at all times of the year, and can be made with any white fish fillets. If you make the terrine in advance, take it out of the fridge 1 hour before serving so that the flavours develop.*

SERVES 6-8

1 tsp sunflower oil
6 young spinach leaves
700 g/1 ½ lb lemon sole fillets, skinned
1 egg
1 egg white
150 ml/5 fl oz whipping cream
¼ tsp paprika
1-2 tbsp lemon juice
salt and freshly ground white pepper
100 g/4 oz cooked peeled prawns
*Sauce*
4 ripe tomatoes, peeled, deseeded and chopped
1 egg yolk
150 ml/5 fl oz Greek-style yogurt
zest and juice of 1 small orange
1 tbsp tomato purée
*Garnish*
2 ripe tomatoes
6 small spinach leaves
6-8 cooked unpeeled prawns (optional)

*1.* Lightly grease a 1.1 litre/2 pint ring mould with oil. Snap off the spinach stems, wash the leaves, pat dry and use them to line the mould.
*2.* Cut the sole into chunks and purée in a food processor until smooth. With the motor running, add the whole egg and egg white, then the cream and paprika and lemon juice to taste. Season with salt and pepper and rub the mixture through a hard sieve to make it really smooth. (This is not absolutely necessary, but it does give a velvety texture.)
*3.* Spoon half the sole mixture into the mould, taking care not to dislodge the spinach leaves. Smooth the surface with a spatula and scatter over the prawns in an even layer. Top with the remaining sole mixture and smooth over the surface.
*4.* Cover the terrine with a sheet of greaseproof paper and cook on MEDIUM for about 8 minutes, until just firm and springy. Leave to stand for 5 minutes.
*5.* Remove the paper and place a wire rack over the mould. Invert the rack and mould on to a shallow dish to catch the juices which will run out of the terrine (keep these to make a fish stock or sauce). Drain for 5-10 minutes, then turn the rack and mould over, remove the rack and unmould the terrine on to a plate.
*6.* To make the sauce, purée the tomatoes, egg yolk, yogurt, orange zest and juice and tomato purée in a food processor until very smooth. Transfer to a bowl and cook on LOW for 3-5 minutes, until slightly thickened, stirring every minute. Stir and chill.
*7.* Meanwhile, prepare the garnish. Peel the tomatoes, deseed and dice finely. Wash the spinach leaves, pat dry and pile them one on top of the other. Roll up tightly into a cigar shape and shred finely.
*8.* To serve, carefully slice the terrine with a serrated knife to reveal the green, pink and white layers, and arrange a slice on each plate. Spoon the sauce round the edge and put a little mould of diced tomato on one side and some shredded spinach on the other. Decorate with a prawn, if you like, and serve at room temperature.

# SMOKED SALMON AND TURBOT TIMBALES

*Serve these pretty timbales either hot or cold as a lunch dish or starter. If you are serving them as a main course, surround them with a garland of attractive salad leaves dressed with a lemony vinaigrette. Turbot has a wonderful flavour, but, alas, it is terribly expensive (although it may become cheaper now that it is being farmed commercially). Until that happy time, trout or cod make good and cheaper alternatives.*

SERVES 4-6

sunflower oil, for greasing
24 sprigs dill
175 g/6 oz smoked salmon slices
450 g/1 lb turbot fillets
2 tbsp dry white wine or vermouth
1 tsp grated lemon zest
100 g/4 oz cream cheese
2 tbsp finely chopped fresh tarragon or chervil (do not use dried)
2 tbsp finely snipped fresh chives
1 egg yolk
salt and freshly ground black pepper
2 egg whites

*1.* Lightly oil 6 ramekins or 4 individual soufflé dishes and lay sprigs of dill in an attractive pattern in each.
*2.* Cut the smoked salmon into 7.5 × 12.5 cm/ 3 × 5 in strips and lay one in each dish, smoothing it down carefully to keep the dill in place. Leave the ends overhanging. Finely shred the smoked salmon trimmings and reserve them.
*3.* Lay the turbot fillets in a shallow dish with the wine or vermouth, cover and cook HIGH for 3-4 minutes, until tender. Leave to stand until cool enough to handle, then discard the skin and flake the flesh.
*4.* Combine the flaked turbot, lemon zest, cream cheese, herbs and egg yolk in a food processor and process until smooth. Season to taste with salt and pepper.
*5.* Heat the egg whites on HIGH for 15 seconds, then whisk until firm but not too dry. Using a metal spoon, carefully fold the whites into the turbot mixture.
*6.* Spoon half the mixture into the prepared dishes. Stir the smoked salmon trimmings into the other half and fill the dishes to the top with this mixture. Fold over the overhanging smoked salmon. Cover and cook on MEDIUM for 2-4 minutes, until just firm and springy. Leave to stand for 5 minutes before turning out, or leave the timbales in the dishes until ready to serve.
*7.* Serve hot or cold with wholemeal bread and unsalted butter.

# GRATIN OF CRAB

*Serve this as a hot starter or an unusual lunch dish. It is nicer made with fresh crab, but frozen white crabmeat will do very well.*

SERVES 4-6

40 g/1 ½ oz butter
2 shallots, finely chopped
100 g/4 oz button mushrooms, thinly sliced
450 g/1 lb cooked white crabmeat
1 tbsp brandy
1 tbsp tomato purée
50 ml/2 fl oz dry sherry
¼ tsp cayenne pepper
salt and freshly ground black pepper
2 tbsp dried brown breadcrumbs

*1.* Put 25 g/1 oz butter into a bowl with the shallots and cook on HIGH for 3 minutes, or until the shallots are soft. Add the mushrooms and cook for a further 2 minutes.
*2.* Add the crabmeat, brandy, tomato purée, sherry, cayenne pepper and salt and pepper to taste and stir well. Spoon the mixture into individual gratin dishes, sprinkle over the bread-crumbs and dot with the remaining butter.
*3.* Cook on COMBINATION 2 for 5-8 minutes, or until browned. Alternatively, put the crab mix-ture into the gratin dishes, cover and microwave on HIGH for 2 minutes. Uncover, sprinkle over the breadcrumbs, dot with butter and brown quickly under a preheated grill.

# SMOKED SALMON QUICHE

*Serve this quiche just warm, accompanied by an elegant green salad of frisée, cornsalad and watercress with a lemony vinaigrette. If you don't have a combination oven, bake the pastry case blind in a conventional oven, then fill and cook in the microwave.*

### SERVES 4

225 g/8 oz shortcrust pastry
butter, for greasing
100 g/4 oz smoked salmon
freshly ground black pepper
300 ml/½ pint single cream
3 eggs
50 ml/2 fl oz milk
freshly grated nutmeg
salt
sprigs of watercress, to garnish

*1.* Roll out the pastry on a floured surface and use it to line a greased 20 cm/8 in flan dish. Place on the low rack and bake blind on COMBINATION 2 for 10-15 minutes, until lightly browned. Alternatively, preheat a conventional oven to 220°C/425°F/Gas mark 7 and bake the pastry case blind for 12-15 minutes. Leave to cool.
*2.* Cut the smoked salmon into thin strips. Reserve a few to decorate the flan, then arrange the rest in the bottom of the flan case and grind over some pepper.
*3.* Beat together the cream, eggs, milk and nutmeg to taste and season with a little salt. Pour the mixture into the flan case, place on the low rack and cook on COMBINATION 2 for 12-15 minutes, until the filling is just set and golden brown. Alternatively, microwave on MEDIUM for 12-16 minutes, rotating the dish a quarter turn every 3 minutes if you do not have a turntable.
*4.* Roll up the reserved salmon strips like 'cigarettes' and arrange them on top of the flan, interspersed with sprigs of watercress. Serve while still warm.

# SOLE WITH CHANTERELLES IN SAFFRON SAUCE

*The glowing orange of the chanterelles combines with the creamy yellow sauce to make a fabulous special lunch dish. Some shops sell broken pieces from the bottom of a basket of chanterelles for little more than the price of cultivated mushrooms – make the most of this bargain! If chanterelles are not available, use oyster mushrooms instead.*

### SERVES 4

4 sole fillets (preferably Dover sole), about
75 g/3 oz each, skinned
4 tbsp Fish stock (see p. 20)
a large pinch of saffron threads
100 g/4 oz chanterelles
1 tbsp butter
4 tbsp double cream
1 egg yolk
salt and freshly ground white pepper

*1.* Halve the sole fillets lengthways and roll them up, skinned side inwards. Arrange them in a shallow serving dish and pour over the fish stock. Cover and cook on HIGH for 3-4 minutes, until the fillets are tender.
*2.* Pour the cooking juices into a jug, add the saffron and cook on HIGH for 1 minute to infuse the flavours. Set aside.
*3.* Briefly wash the chanterelles to remove any bits of twig or fern, drain well and quarter any that are large. Place in a bowl with the butter and cook on HIGH for 2 minutes until just tender.
*4.* Add the cream to the saffron-flavoured stock and heat on HIGH for 30 seconds. Lightly beat the egg yolk with a fork, pour in a little hot sauce and stir well, then stir it back into the rest of the sauce. Season to taste with salt and pepper and cook on MEDIUM for 30 seconds, until slightly thickened. Stir in the chanterelles and pour the golden sauce over the sole fillets. Serve at once.

Sole with Chanterelles in Saffron Sauce

# BRANDIED SALMON MOUSSE

*This wonderful cold mousse makes a little salmon go a long way. If brandy seems a trifle too alcoholic at lunchtime, substitute dry white wine or sherry.*

SERVES 6

225 g/8 oz salmon fillet
75 ml/3 fl oz Fish stock (see p. 20)
15 g/½ oz powdered gelatine
2 tsp lemon juice
1 ½ tbsp brandy, dry white wine or dry sherry
2 tbsp freshly grated Parmesan cheese
300 ml/½ pint whipping cream
salt and freshly ground white pepper
2 egg whites
sunflower oil, for greasing
*Garnish*
¼ cucumber, unpeeled and very finely sliced
sprigs of chervil

*1.* Put the salmon into a dish with the fish stock, cover and cook on HIGH for 2-3 minutes, until just cooked. Strain the stock into a jug and leave the fish to cool.
*2.* Stir the gelatine into the hot stock until dissolved. If necessary, heat on HIGH for about 15 seconds to dissolve it completely.
*3.* When the salmon is cool enough to handle, discard the skin and flake the flesh. Pour the gelatine and stock into a blender or food processor and start the motor. Gradually add the flaked salmon, lemon juice, brandy, wine or sherry and Parmesan cheese and process until smooth. Leave to cool.
*4.* Lightly whip the cream, then carefully fold in the cooled salmon mixture (make sure it is cool or the cream may separate). Season to taste with salt and pepper, cover and chill until the mixture is just beginning to set, but is still quite liquid.
*5.* Put the egg whites into the bowl of an electric mixer, or similar bowl, and heat on HIGH for 15-20 seconds to warm them slightly. Do not worry if they just begin to set at the edges; warming them will greatly increase their volume when they are beaten. Beat them with a pinch of salt until soft peaks form, then, using a metal spoon, fold them lightly into the salmon mixture.
*6.* Turn the mousse into a lightly greased soufflé dish or individual ramekins and chill in the fridge until set. Just before serving, arrange overlapping slices of cucumber around the edge of the mousse and put some sprigs of chervil in the middle.

# SMOKED FISH SURPRISE

*This elegant mousse takes surprisingly little time to prepare, but looks very special, studded with layers of smoked salmon and asparagus. Use fresh or frozen asparagus, if possible, although canned spears will do at a pinch.*

SERVES 6-8

12 fresh asparagus spears
100 g/4 oz smoked salmon
1 tbsp powdered gelatine
juice of ½ lemon
150 ml/5 fl oz Fish stock (see p. 20)
50 g/2 oz butter
2 shallots, finely chopped
100 ml/3½ fl oz soured cream
225 g/8 oz smoked trout fillets
225 g/8 oz cottage cheese
1 egg white
12 spinach leaves
lemon triangles, to garnish

*1.* Put the asparagus and 2 tbsp water into a dish, cover and cook on HIGH for 5-7 minutes, until the spears are tender but still crisp. Drain and set aside. Cut the smoked salmon into long strips.
*2.* Stir the gelatine into the lemon juice, add the fish stock, cover and cook on HIGH for about 1 minute, until the gelatine has dissolved completely, stirring halfway through. Stir and put on one side.
*3.* Put the butter and shallots into a large bowl, cover and cook on HIGH for 2 minutes to soften the shallots. Cool slightly, then place in a blender or food processor with the soured cream, stock mixture, smoked trout fillets and cottage cheese.

Process until smooth. Beat the egg white until soft peaks form and fold it gently into the mixture, then chill in the fridge.

4. Wash the spinach, remove the stalks and cook the leaves on HIGH for 1 minute. Refresh in cold water, drain and pat dry. Line a 1.1 litre/2 pint rectangular terrine with clingfilm, then with the spinach leaves. Carefully spread one-third of the smoked trout mousse over the spinach, put in the asparagus spears and cover with another one-third of the mousse.

5. Arrange the smoked salmon lengthways on the mousse and finish with another layer of mousse. Fold any overhanging spinach leaves back over the mousse, cover with clingfilm and chill for at least 4 hours.

6. Turn out the mousse on to a serving dish, carefully peel off the clingfilm and garnish with lemon triangles.

# CRÊPES EN MOUCLADE

*This elegant pancake layer can be sandwiched with any fishy mixture and is particularly delicious filled with a creamy mussel sauce.*

### SERVES 6

1.75 g/4 lb mussels, scrubbed and debearded
150 ml/5 fl oz dry white wine
a pinch of saffron threads or ½ tsp saffron powder
3 shallots or 1 onion, finely chopped
1 clove garlic, crushed
50 g/2 oz butter
2 tbsp plain flour
salt and freshly ground white pepper
100 ml/3 ½ fl oz double cream
1 egg yolk
2 tbsp finely chopped fresh parsley
12 thin savoury pancakes
25 g/1 oz Gruyère cheese, grated

1. Put half the mussels and all the wine and saffron into a large bowl and cook on HIGH for 3-5 minutes, until all the mussels have opened, shaking the bowl occasionally and stirring half-way through. Discard any which do not open. Lift out the cooked mussels with a slotted spoon and cook the rest in the same way.

2. Remove the mussels from their shells and chop them roughly. Strain the cooking liquid into a jug.

3. Put the onion, garlic and butter into a bowl and cook on HIGH for 3-4 minutes. Stir in the flour and cook on HIGH for 1 minute, then whisk in the mussel stock and cook on HIGH for 3-5 minutes, or until thickened. Season to taste.

4. Lightly whisk together the cream and egg yolk and pour in a little of the hot sauce. Pour the mixture back into the sauce, whisk, then cook on MEDIUM for 2-3 minutes, until the sauce is very thick and creamy. Do not let it boil. Stir in half the parsley, then the chopped mussels.

5. Stack up the pancakes and sauce in layers, keeping a little sauce to cover the top pancake. Sprinkle with grated Gruyère and cook on HIGH for about 1 minute, until the cheese has melted. Scatter over the remaining parsley and serve.

In this chapter you will find a wide variety of fish dishes, ranging from the classics, such as Sole Véronique and Skate with black butter and capers to recipes which make the most of those exotic fish, like red snapper and golden sea bream, which are now finding their way into the markets.

Do not worry if you cannot find the fish specified in the recipe; another variety will usually do just as well. Be guided by what fish looks freshest or any seasonal bargains when you go shopping and adapt the recipes to suit the fish you buy.

Most fish is best served with plainly cooked, crisp vegetables or salads which provide a contrast of flavour and texture; do not swamp a delicate fish or shellfish with complicated or highly seasoned accompaniments. Offset white fish with fresh, brightly coloured vegetables; plain steamed cauliflower or salsify may taste fine, but the assembled dish will look pallid on the plate.

Most of the dishes in this chapter will serve four or six people, but they can easily be adapted to serve only one or two; just adjust the ingredients as appropriate and cut the cooking time proportionately. Half quantities will need slightly less than half the specified cooking time and quarter quantities less than one-quarter. If the fish seems underdone, give it a few seconds more, but be sure to check it every 20 seconds after the calculated cooking time. Remember that small quantities of fish cook very quickly – often in less than a minute. Do not be tempted to cook more fish than you need for one meal; it really does not take kindly to being reheated.

# MAIN COURSES

CHAPTER 5

# POACHED MACKEREL WITH GOOSEBERRY SAUCE

*This method is suitable for any whole fish. If you like, leave the fish to cool in the poaching liquid and serve cold with Mayonnaise (see p. 25) or Herb and yogurt sauce (see p. 21). To poach 1 or 2 fish, reduce the poaching liquid ingredients by half and cook for 4-6 minutes per 450 g/1 lb.*

### SERVES 4

1 carrot, finely sliced
1 celery stalk, finely sliced
½ lemon, sliced
1 bay leaf
4 white peppercorns
2 parsley stalks
1 sprig thyme
50 ml/2 fl oz dry white wine or vermouth
100 ml/3 ½ fl oz water
4 mackerel, about 250 g/9 oz each, cleaned
Gooseberry sauce, to serve (see p. 23)

*1.* Place all the ingredients except the fish and sauce in a large shallow dish. Cover and cook on HIGH for 10 minutes to make a court bouillon.
*2.* Arrange the fish on top of the vegetables and herbs, cover and cook on HIGH for 8-10 minutes, until the flesh becomes opaque, rotating the dish halfway through if your microwave does not have a turntable.
*3.* Leave to stand for 5 minutes, then serve the mackerel with gooseberry sauce. Keep the poaching liquid to use another time; it will keep in the freezer for at least a month.

# SALMON AND SCALLOP KEBABS

*Succulent salmon and scallops are combined to make a quick but elegant dish. The kebabs can be assembled in advance and microwaved at the last moment. Serve them on a bed of saffron rice.*

### SERVES 4

225 g/8 oz salmon fillet, skinned
4 large or 8 small shelled scallops with their corals
8 baby onions
½ red pepper, deseeded and cut into 8 pieces
15 g/½ oz butter
juice of ½ lemon
a pinch of paprika
*Sauce*
50 g/2 oz butter
1 tsp chopped fresh tarragon
1 tbsp dry vermouth
salt and freshly ground white pepper

*1.* Cut the salmon into twelve 2.5-cm/1-in cubes. Halve the large scallops (leave small ones whole) and prick the corals twice with a cocktail stick to prevent them from bursting.
*2.* Thread the salmon, scallops, corals, onions and red pepper on to four 23-cm/9-in wooden skewers and place in a shallow dish. Cover with greaseproof paper.
*3.* Melt the butter on HIGH for about 30 seconds, add lemon juice and paprika to taste and brush over the kebabs.
*4.* Make the sauce before cooking the kebabs so that you can use it to baste them. Put the butter in a bowl and cook on HIGH for about 1 minute, until melted. Whisk in the tarragon and vermouth and season to taste with salt and pepper.
*5.* Cook the kebabs on HIGH for 4-6 minutes, or until the fish and scallops are just tender, turning and basting them with the sauce every 2 minutes. Reheat the remaining sauce on HIGH for 1 minute, stir well and serve separately.

# HALIBUT BANGKOK

*The inspiration for this aromatic fish stew came from Thailand, where the food is subtly spiced yet often mind-blowingly hot. You can always reduce the number of chillies if you prefer, although their fiery flavour is tempered by the creamy coconut milk. If coconut milk proves hard to find, you can make your own by stirring 600 ml/1 pint boiling water into 75 g/3 oz creamed coconut.*

SERVES 4

4 halibut or any firm white fish cutlets, about
225 g/8 oz each
600 ml/1 pint coconut milk
1 tbsp finely chopped lemon grass or 2 tsp grated
lime zest
2-3 fresh red or green chillies, deseeded and thinly
sliced
1-2 tsp fresh lime juice
1-2 tbsp light soy sauce
steamed rice, to serve
2 spring onions, finely chopped
2 tbsp finely chopped fresh coriander

*1.* Put the fish into a shallow dish and pour over the coconut milk. Stir in the lemon grass or lime zest, cover and cook on HIGH for 6-8 minutes, until the fish is just tender.
*2.* Stir in the sliced chillies and add lime juice and soy sauce to taste. Cover and cook on HIGH for 1-2 minutes.
*3.* Lay the fish on a bed of rice in a deep serving dish and spoon over some of the sauce. Scatter over the spring onions and coriander and serve at once. Serve the remaining sauce separately.

# SEA SYMPHONY

*Serve this glorious medley of fish in deep soup plates and provide plenty of French bread to mop up the sauce. Any firm fish fillets can be used, but try to choose at least two varieties of fish with attractive skins, as they make the dish look very pretty. If you can't find samphire, substitute asparagus tips or fine French beans.*

SERVES 6

225 g/8 oz turbot or halibut fillet, skinned
225 g/8 oz sole fillets, skinned
225 g/8 oz sea bream fillet, scaled
225 g/8 oz sea bass fillet, scaled
1 red mullet, about 225 g/8 oz, scaled and filleted
100 g/4 oz samphire or 12 fresh asparagus tips
150 ml/5 fl oz Fish stock (see p. 20)
150 ml/5 fl oz dry white wine
a pinch of saffron threads
50 g/2 oz butter, chilled and diced
salt and freshly ground white pepper

*1.* Cut all the fish into 5 × 2 cm/2 × ¾ in strips.
*2.* Put the samphire or asparagus tips into a dish with 2 tbsp water, cover and cook on HIGH for 2-3 minutes, until just tender. Drain and set aside.
*3.* Arrange the fish in a single layer in a dish and pour over the fish stock and wine. Cover and cook on HIGH for 5-7 minutes until barely tender. Carefully strain the poaching liquid into a saucepan. Cover the fish and keep warm while you make the sauce.
*4.* Add the saffron to the poaching liquid and boil over high heat until the liquid is reduced by about one-third. Take the pan off the heat and beat in the butter, one piece at a time, until the sauce is very smooth. Season to taste with salt and pepper.
*5.* Using a slotted spoon, arrange the fish in the soup plates, skin side upwards, making sure that everyone has a little of each type of fish. Pour the sauce over and scatter each serving with samphire or asparagus. Serve at once.

# SEA BREAM WITH FENNEL

*Many not terribly flavoursome fish masquerade under the guise of bream; what you need for this dish is golden sea bream (daurade in French). If you cannot find sea bream, substitute with any whole firm white fish.*

### SERVES 4

2 fennel bulbs, cut into strips
1 tbsp olive oil
1 whole sea bream, about 900 g/2 lb, scaled and cleaned
salt and freshly ground black pepper
1 sprig thyme
1 bay leaf
3 tbsp Court bouillon (see p. 20)
1 tbsp Pernod (optional)
fennel fronds, to garnish

*1.* Put the fennel and oil into a shallow dish large enough to take the fish. Cover and cook on HIGH for about 5 minutes, or until the fennel is almost tender but still slightly crisp.
*2.* Season the sea bream with salt and pepper and stuff the inside with the thyme and bay leaf. Lay the fish on top of the fennel, pour over the court bouillon and Pernod, if using. Cover the dish and cook on HIGH for about 8-10 minutes (depending on the thickness of the bream), until the flesh comes away easily from the bone.
*3.* Arrange the bream on a serving dish with the cooked fennel around the edge. Spoon over the cooking juices, decorate lavishly with fennel fronds and serve.

# RED MULLET FILLED WITH CRAB

*Red mullet have a delicate flavour which marries well with crab. Be sure to scale the fish before cooking, or the texture will be spoilt. If possible, keep their livers to add to the stuffing – they are delicious. You can also cook grey mullet in this way, but they will not look as pretty and their livers are not worth eating.*

### SERVES 4

1 tbsp olive oil
2 tomatoes, skinned, deseeded and diced
1 celery stalk, chopped
½ green pepper, deseeded and chopped
2 shallots or 1 small onion, chopped
200 g/7 oz white crabmeat
livers from the red mullet (optional)
1 tbsp chopped fresh chervil
1 tbsp chopped fresh coriander
1 tsp Tabasco sauce
1 tsp lemon juice
salt and freshly ground white pepper
4 red mullet, about 175 g/6 oz each, cleaned and scaled
*Garnish*
sprigs of chervil
lemon and lime slices

*1.* Combine the oil, tomatoes, celery, green pepper and shallots or onion in a bowl. Cover and cook on HIGH for 3-4 minutes, until the vegetables are tender, stirring halfway through. Drain.
*2.* Stir in the crabmeat, mullet livers, chervil and coriander and season with Tabasco sauce, lemon juice, salt and pepper. Stuff the red mullet with this mixture.
*3.* Arrange the fish in a shallow dish, alternating them top to tail. Cover and cook on HIGH for 8-10 minutes, giving the dish a half turn every 2 minutes. The red mullet flesh should be opaque.
*4.* Leave to stand for 5 minutes, then serve, garnished with sprigs of chervil and lemon slices.

*Top:* Sea Bream with Fennel
*Bottom:* Red Mullet Filled with Crab

# TROUT ST MALO

*If you can find flavourful little brown shrimps, use them for this recipe. Just remove the heads and whiskers, but do not shell them; the shells add a deliciously crunchy texture.*

SERVES 2

75 g/3 oz butter
75 g/3 oz dried white breadcrumbs
100 g/4 oz shrimps
grated zest and juice of 1 lemon
1 tbsp snipped fresh chives or chopped parsley
1 egg, beaten
salt and freshly ground black pepper
2 trout, about 350 g/12 oz each, cleaned
*Garnish*
lemon twists
sprigs of flat-leaved parsley

*1.* Put the butter into a bowl and cook on HIGH for about 2 minutes, until melted. Keep a little aside to brush over the trout. Stir the breadcrumbs, shrimps, lemon zest and juice and herbs into the remaining butter, then add the egg and mix well. Season to taste with salt and pepper.
*2.* Stuff the cavities of the trout with the mixture and arrange the fish in a dish. Brush them with the reserved melted butter, place the dish on the grill rack and cook on COMBINATION 5 for 7-10 minutes, until the trout is tender and golden brown. Alternatively, cover the dish and microwave on HIGH for 7-9 minutes, until tender. Leave to stand for 5 minutes before serving.
*3.* Garnish with lemon twists and parsley sprigs and serve.

# ESCALOPES OF SALMON WITH SORREL AND MADEIRA

*The salmon must be barely cooked in this wonderful dish, which is adapted from one of the classic* nouvelle cuisine *recipes. The sharpness of sorrel contrasts perfectly with the Madeira; if sorrel is not available use spinach instead and add the juice of half a lemon to the sauce.*

SERVES 4

2 salmon fillets, about 250 g/9 oz each, skinned
75 g/3 oz fresh sorrel, trimmed and washed
2 shallots, finely chopped
300 ml/½ pint Fish stock (see p. 20)
6 tbsp dry Madeira
300 ml/½ pint double cream
40 g/1 ½ oz butter, diced
salt and freshly ground white pepper
2 tbsp dry white wine

*1.* Slice the salmon fillets horizontally through the middle to make 4 thin escalopes. Lay them between 2 sheets of clingfilm and flatten gently with a steak mallet until they are of an even thickness. Roughly shred the sorrel leaves.
*2.* In a large bowl, combine the chopped shallots, fish stock and Madeira and cook on HIGH for 15-20 minutes, until syrupy and reduced by half. Stir in the cream and cook on HIGH for 2-3 minutes, until the sauce has thickened slightly.
*3.* Stir in the sorrel, cook on HIGH for 15 seconds, then, using a wooden spoon, beat in the diced butter one piece at a time until the sauce is smooth and rich. Season to taste with salt and pepper and set aside.
*4.* Lay the salmon escalopes in a single layer in a shallow dish, skinned side down. Sprinkle over the wine, cover and cook on HIGH for 2-3 minutes, until the salmon is barely cooked.
*5.* Spoon the sauce on to 4 warmed plates and, using a fish slice, carefully place a salmon escalope in the middle of each plate. Serve immediately.

# SOLE IN CIDER

*This unusual combination of flavours also works well with other flat fish fillets. Be sure to use dry cider (preferably farmhouse).*

SERVES 4

2 sole, about 700 g/1½ lb each, or 4 small sole, filleted
300 ml/½ pint dry cider
½ dessert apple (Granny Smith or Cox), peeled and cut into 8 slices
25 g/1 oz butter, softened
1 tbsp plain flour
lemon juice
salt and freshly ground white pepper
1 tbsp finely chopped fresh parsley
4 tbsp double cream

*1.* Lay the sole fillets in a dish, with the thinner ends tucked under. Pour over the cider, cover and cook on HIGH for about 6 minutes, or until the sole is just tender.
*2.* Transfer the fish to a serving dish and keep warm while you make the sauce. Put the dish containing the cider back in the microwave and cook on HIGH for about 5 minutes, until the cider is slightly reduced
*3.* Put the apple slices in the cider, cover and cook on HIGH for 2-3 minutes, until just tender. Remove the apple with a slotted spoon and set aside.
*4.* Mash together the butter and flour to make a smooth paste and whisk this into the cider, a little at a time, until smooth. Cook on HIGH for 2-3 minutes, until the sauce is thickened and smooth, whisking every minute.
*5.* Season to taste with lemon juice, salt and pepper, then stir in the parsley and cream and pour the sauce over the sole fillets. Garnish with the poached apple slices and serve at once.

# CARNIVAL KEBABS

*Serve these colourful kebabs on a bed of rice mixed with sweetcorn and petits pois. When cherry tomatoes are not in season, substitute small wedges of red pepper. If you do not like smoked fish, fresh cod or halibut make good alternatives.*

SERVES 4

4 smoked haddock or cod fillets, skinned
3 small courgettes
12 small button mushrooms, wiped and trimmed
12 cherry tomatoes
8 small bay leaves
2 tbsp sunflower oil
1 tbsp lemon juice
1 tbsp chopped fresh parsley
1 tsp fresh thyme or ½ tsp dried thyme
freshly ground black pepper
*Garnish*
lemon wedges (optional)
sprigs of parsley (optional)

*1.* Cut the fish fillets into 1-cm/½-in cubes. Top and tail the courgettes, trim them down their length all the way round with a cannelle knife to give a striped effect and cut each into 8 chunks.
*2.* Thread the fish, courgettes, mushrooms, tomatoes and bay leaves on to 8 wooden skewers, alternating the different ingredients to give an attractive variety of colours.
*3.* In a large shallow dish, whisk together the oil, lemon juice and herbs. Turn the kebabs in this mixture so that they are well coated, then season with pepper. Cover with a sheet of greaseproof paper and cook on HIGH for 3 minutes. Turn the kebabs and brush with the cooking juices, then re-cover and cook on HIGH for another 2-3 minutes, or until the fish is tender.
*4.* Garnish with lemon wedges and parsley sprigs, if using, and serve very hot.

# JAMBALAYA

*The joy of this colourful Creole dish is that you can use almost any fish, poultry and shellfish to create a tasty and attractive one-pot meal.*

### SERVES 6

1 onion, coarsely chopped
2 celery stalks, coarsely chopped
1-2 cloves garlic, finely chopped
1 tbsp sunflower or corn oil
350 g/12 oz long grain rice
a pinch of cayenne pepper
600 ml/1 pint boiling chicken stock (a cube is fine)
1 red pepper, deseeded and diced
1 green pepper, deseeded and diced
100 g/4 oz canned okra, drained
400 g/14 oz tomato passata
salt and freshly ground black pepper
100 g/4 oz cooked fish or chicken, diced
100 g/4 oz ham, in one piece, diced
225 g/8 oz cooked unpeeled prawns
200 g/7 oz can clams, cockles or mussels
2 tbsp chopped fresh parsley, to garnish

*1.* Combine the onion, celery, garlic and oil in a large bowl or casserole and cook on HIGH for 3-4 minutes, until the vegetables are soft. Stir in the rice and cayenne pepper, then pour in the boiling stock. Cover and cook on HIGH for 10-12 minutes, until all the liquid has been absorbed, but the rice still has some 'bite'.
*2.* Stir in the red and green peppers, okra and tomato passata and leave to stand for 5 minutes. Season to taste with salt and pepper, then stir in the cooked fish or chicken, ham and shellfish. Cover and cook on HIGH for 5 minutes until the jambalaya is heated through, stirring twice.
*3.* Pile it on to a warm serving dish, sprinkle with parsley and serve at once.

*Left:* Carnival Kebabs (page 77)
*Right:* Jambalaya

# SAVOURY PLAICE ROLLS

*Try to persuade the fishmonger to skin the plaice fillets for you, as it is a fiddly (though not difficult) job. Keep the bones and heads to make a fish stock.*

SERVES 4

8 small plaice fillets, about 450 g/1 lb, skinned
50 g/2 oz butter
4 tbsp Fish stock (see p. 20)
1 tbsp snipped fresh chives
sprigs of parsley, to garnish
*Stuffing*
4 spring onions, finely chopped
25 g/1 oz butter
6 tbsp fresh brown breadcrumbs
50 g/2 oz almonds, chopped
finely grated zest and juice of 1 orange
2 tbsp chopped fresh parsley
½ tsp chopped fresh thyme
1 tbsp tomato purée
salt and freshly ground black pepper

*1.* First make the stuffing; put the spring onions and butter into a large bowl, cover and cook on HIGH for 2 minutes to soften the onions. Stir in the rest of the stuffing ingredients, seasoning to taste with salt and pepper.
*2.* Lay the plaice fillets, skinned-side up, on a plate, spread the stuffing over them and roll up, starting from the tail end. Secure with wooden cocktail sticks and arrange in a shallow dish.
*3.* Put the butter into a small bowl and cook on HIGH for about 1 minute, or until melted. Stir in the fish stock and chives and season. Pour over the fish, cover the dish and cook on HIGH for 7-8 minutes, until the fish is tender, turning the dish halfway through. Decorate the rolls with parsley sprigs and serve.

# SOLE FLORENTINE

*The microwave prepares this classic dish to perfection, retaining all the fresh flavours of the spinach and sole. Plaice fillets are equally good cooked in this way, and you can use frozen spinach if necessary.*

SERVES 4

700 g/1 ½ lb fresh spinach
25 g/1 oz butter
1 small onion, finely chopped
grated zest of ½ lemon
1 tbsp wholegrain mustard
salt and freshly ground black pepper
700 g/1½ lb sole fillets, skinned
2 tbsp freshly grated Parmesan cheese

*1.* Wash the spinach, discard the stalks and cook the leaves on HIGH with no added water for 3-4 minutes, stirring halfway through. Drain well and chop coarsely.
*2.* Put half the butter, the onion, lemon zest and mustard into a large bowl. Cover and cook on HIGH for 3 minutes, until the onion is soft. Stir in the chopped spinach and season to taste with salt and pepper.
*3.* Spread the spinach mixture over the bottom of a serving dish, arrange the sole fillets on top in a single layer and dot with the remaining butter. Cover and microwave on HIGH for 5-7 minutes, rearranging the fillets after 3 minutes so that they cook evenly.
*4.* Sprinkle over the Parmesan and cook on HIGH for 2 minutes, or brown under a medium hot grill. Leave to stand for 3 minutes before serving.

# SEAFOOD CRÊPES

*Serve one of these fish-filled pancakes as a starter, or two as a main course. If you haven't got a combination oven, prepare and heat the filled pancakes in the microwave, and then brown the cheese under the grill.*

SERVES 4

225 g/8 oz pink trout, cod or haddock fillets
100 g/4 oz button mushrooms, thinly sliced
100 ml/3 ½ fl oz dry white wine
25 g/1 oz butter, plus extra for greasing
1 onion, finely chopped
2 tbsp plain flour
a pinch of saffron powder (optional)
150 ml/5 fl oz milk
1 tbsp lemon juice
4 tbsp double cream
salt and freshly ground white pepper
100 g/4 oz cooked peeled prawns
8 thin 20 cm/8 in savoury pancakes
4 tbsp grated Gruyère cheese
*Garnish*
sprigs of parsley
lemon wedges

*1.* Put the fish fillets and sliced mushrooms into a shallow dish with the wine, cover and cook on HIGH for 2-3 minutes, until the fish is tender. Leave to rest while you make the sauce.
*2.* Meanwhile, put 25 g/1 oz butter and the chopped onion into a bowl and cook on HIGH for 2-3 minutes to soften the onion.
*3.* Stir in the flour, saffron, if using, milk and lemon juice, then strain the cooking liquid from the fish into the mixture and stir well. Cover and cook on HIGH for 2 minutes; stir well and cook for another 2 minutes, until the sauce has thickened. Add the cream and season to taste with salt and freshly ground white pepper.
*4.* Remove the skin from the fillets and flake the flesh. Carefully stir the flaked fish, mushrooms and prawns into the sauce.
*5.* Generously butter an ovenproof dish. Divide the fish mixture between the pancakes, roll them up, or fold over, and arrange in the dish.

*6.* Sprinkle over the cheese and cook on COMBINATION 2 for 10-12 minutes, until bubbling and golden. Alternatively, microwave the filled pancakes on HIGH for about 3 minutes to heat through, then place under a medium hot grill until the cheese is melted and browned.

# SALMON STEAKS WITH ORANGE BUTTER SAUCE

*Now that good farmed salmon is available, this delicious dish is no longer a monstrous extravagance. Serve the salmon with minted new potatoes and French beans for a taste of simple luxury. Pink trout fillets make a good alternative.*

SERVES 4

4 salmon steaks, about 225 g/8 oz each
4 tbsp dry white wine
1 small orange (Seville, if possible), thinly sliced
4 small sprigs tarragon
salt and freshly ground white pepper
Orange butter sauce, to serve (see p. 23)
*Garnish*
finely shredded orange zest
1 orange slice, quartered

*1.* Arrange the salmon steaks in a shallow dish, with the thinner ends towards the centre of the dish.
*2.* Pour over the wine and arrange the orange slices around the fish. Top each steak with a sprig of tarragon. Cover and cook on HIGH for 6-8 minutes, until the salmon is just tender and still a bright pink. Uncover, season lightly with salt and pepper, and leave to stand for 5 minutes.
*3.* Arrange the steaks on individual plates and spoon a little orange butter sauce at the side. Garnish each one with shredded zest and a quarter of an orange slice.

# SCALLOPS WITH WILD MUSHROOMS

*I invented this dish when a generous Frenchman gave me a bag of wonderful assorted wild mushrooms. If you aren't lucky enough to find fresh fungi, use dried Italian funghi porcini and soak them in warm water for 30 minutes before using. Keep the water to use for stocks or soups.*

SERVES 2-4

4 large shelled scallops, with their corals
50 g/2 oz wild mushrooms (chanterelles, mousserons or even oyster or field mushrooms), trimmed and washed
25 g/1 oz butter
50 ml/2 fl oz dry vermouth
50 ml/2 fl oz double cream
salt and freshly ground black pepper
1 egg yolk, lightly beaten
new potatoes, mange-tout, broccoli florets and baby carrots, to serve

*1.* Cut the scallops into 5-mm/¼-in slices and prick the corals twice with a cocktail stick. If the mushrooms are large, cut them into even-sized pieces so that they cook evenly.
*2.* Heat a browning dish on HIGH for 5-8 minutes, or according to the manufacturer's instructions, then quickly rub the butter over the dish. It will sizzle and turn brown. Turn the scallop slices and corals in the hot butter, then transfer them to a plate, cover with another plate and set aside.
*3.* Put the prepared mushrooms in the browning dish and cook on HIGH for 2 minutes, or until just tender, stirring after 1 minute. Pour in the vermouth and cook on HIGH for 2 minutes. Add the cream, season to taste with salt and pepper and cook on HIGH for 1 minute, until the sauce begins to thicken.
*4.* Stir in the scallops and the juices they have released during resting. Spoon a little of the sauce into the beaten egg yolk, then pour the mixture back into the dish, pile the mushrooms on top of the scallops and cook on MEDIUM for 2-3

minutes, until the scallops are just cooked and the sauce has thickened slightly.
*5.* Spoon the scallops and mushrooms into the centre of your serving plates, pour over the sauce and serve surrounded by a bouquet of tender young vegetables.

# CARIBBEAN SNAPPER

*Exotic red snapper is readily available nowadays and adds a note of authenticity to this dish. If you can't find snapper, substitute ocean perch, which also has an attractive reddish-gold skin.*

SERVES 4

2 tbsp desiccated coconut
¼ tsp curry powder
15 g/½ oz butter
700 g/1 ½ lb red snapper fillets
2 tbsp mango chutney
freshly ground black pepper
saffron rice, to serve
1 small ripe fresh mango, peeled and thinly sliced, to garnish

*1.* Put the coconut, curry powder and butter into a shallow dish and cook on HIGH for 1-2 minutes, until golden.
*2.* Cut the snapper into 4 portions and spread with mango chutney. Arrange them in a shallow dish, with the thickest parts outwards, grind over some black pepper and pour over the coconut and butter mixture.
*3.* Cover and cook on HIGH for 3 minutes, then rearrange the fish fillets, re-cover and cook for another 4-5 minutes, until tender. Leave to stand for 5 minutes, then serve the snapper fillets on a bed of saffron rice, with the fresh mango slices fanned out beside them.

Scallops with Wild Mushrooms

# FILLETS OF BRILL À LA GRECQUE

*Brill is a flat fish, which looks rather like a turbot, but has a less fine flavour. It needs a fairly robust sauce like this one from Greece to give it character.*

SERVES 4

2 tsp coriander seeds, crushed
1 tsp celery seeds, crushed
2 tbsp olive oil
1 clove garlic, crushed
1 onion, finely chopped
1 celery stalk, finely chopped
400 g/14 oz can tomatoes
1 sprig thyme
1 bay leaf
150 ml/5 fl oz dry white wine
salt and freshly ground black pepper
4 brill fillets, about 200 g/7 oz each
1 lemon, thinly sliced
12 small black olives
2 tbsp chopped fresh parsley, to garnish

*1.* Combine the coriander and celery seeds in a bowl with the oil, garlic, onion, celery, tomatoes, herbs and wine. Cook on HIGH for about 10 minutes, until the sauce is reduced and slightly thickened. Remove the herbs and season the sauce with salt and pepper.
*2.* Arrange the brill fillets in a shallow dish and pour the sauce over the top. Arrange the lemon slices and olives on top, cover and cook on HIGH for 7-9 minutes, or until the fish is tender.
*3.* Sprinkle with chopped parsley and serve.

# MALAYSIAN FISH CURRY

*It is essential to use a firm-fleshed fish for this aromatic curry or it will disintegrate during cooking. If you can find shark steaks, they are ideal, otherwise cod, huss and grey mullet are all suitable.*

SERVES 4-6

1 cm/½ in cube of tamarind or finely grated zest and juice of 1 lime
2 tbsp coriander seeds
½ tsp cumin seeds
½ tsp fennel seeds
½ tsp ground turmeric
3 dried red chillies
1 large onion, finely chopped
1-2 cloves garlic, finely chopped
1 cm/½ in piece of ginger root, peeled and crushed
176 ml/6 fl oz coconut milk
(see Halibut Bangkok, p. 73)
salt
700 g/1½ lb firm fish steaks or cutlets
steamed rice, to serve
4 spring onions, chopped to garnish

*1.* Soak the tamarind in 100 ml/3½ fl oz warm water.
*2.* Finely grind all the dried spices in a blender. Add the chopped onion, garlic, crushed ginger and coconut milk and blend until smooth.
*3.* Pour the mixture into a casserole and cook on HIGH for 2-3 minutes, until boiling. Reduce the power to MEDIUM and simmer for 5 minutes to blend all the flavours.
*4.* Strain the tamarind soaking water through a metal sieve into the sauce, pressing on the tamarind to extract as much juice as possible, or stir in the lime zest and juice. Season the sauce with salt to taste, then put the fish in the casserole in a single layer and spoon the sauce over the top. Cover and cook on HIGH for 6-8 minutes (shark will take a few minutes longer), until the fish is tender.
*5.* Arrange the fish curry on a bed of steamed rice, scatter over the chopped spring onions and serve very hot.

# JOHN DORY BOULANGÈRE

*John Dory is becoming more widely available in Britain, but if it is hard to find, this simple French peasant dish is still delicious made with other fish like sole, halibut or turbot. Use waxy salad potatoes for this dish, or they will disintegrate during cooking.*

SERVES 6

1.5 kg/3-3 ½ lb John Dory, cleaned, or 6 fillets
100 g/4 oz butter
2 large onions, thinly sliced
2 cloves garlic, finely chopped
900 g/2 lb waxy potatoes, very thinly sliced
salt and freshly ground black pepper
150 ml/5 fl oz chicken stock
2 tsp chopped fresh thyme or ½ tsp dried thyme
thyme flowers or chopped fresh herbs, to garnish

*1.* If you are using a whole fish, trim the fins and tail with scissors.
*2.* Put half the butter into a deep dish with the sliced onions and cook on HIGH for 4-5 minutes, until the onions are soft and turning golden. Stir in the garlic.
*3.* Spread the onions over the bottom of a shallow dish and lay the fish on top. Cover with the sliced potatoes and season to taste with salt and pepper.
*4.* Heat the chicken stock on HIGH for 3-4 minutes, until boiling, and pour it over the potatoes. Melt the remaining butter on HIGH for 1-2 minutes and pour it over the assembled dish.
*5.* Sprinkle the thyme over the top, cover and cook on MEDIUM for 20-25 minutes, until the fish and potatoes are tender. Sprinkle with thyme flowers or a mixture of chopped fresh herbs and serve straight from the dish.

# TROUT WITH PINE NUTS

*A variation on the theme of trout with almonds. Only use pink-fleshed trout for this recipe as the flavour is much better than white-fleshed trout.*

SERVES 2

2 rainbow trout, about 350 g/12 oz each, cleaned
1 tbsp lemon juice
salt and freshly ground white pepper
50 g/2 oz pine nuts
50 g/2 oz butter
*Garnish*
sprigs of parsley
lemon wedges

*1.* Heat a browning dish on HIGH for 5-8 minutes, or according to the manufacturer's instructions.
*2.* Sprinkle the trout with lemon juice and lightly season the insides with salt and pepper.
*3.* Put the pine nuts and butter in the heated browning dish and cook on HIGH for 2-3 minutes, until golden brown, stirring halfway through. Transfer the pine nuts to a plate and set aside.
*4.* Put the trout in the browning dish and cook on HIGH for 3 minutes, then carefully turn them over with a fish slice and cook on HIGH for another 3-4 minutes, until the flesh comes easily away from the bone.
*5.* Pour the pine nuts over the trout. Garnish with parsley and lemon and serve.

# MOULES PROVENÇALES

*Serve this dish from the south of France with hot French bread and a very necessary fingerbowl of warm water!*

SERVES 4

225 g/8 oz unsmoked streaky bacon
2.25 kg/5 lb mussels, scrubbed and debearded
100 ml/3½ fl oz dry white wine
4 tbsp chopped fresh parsley
4 tbsp freshly grated Parmesan cheese
chopped fresh parsley, to garnish
*Provençal sauce*
1 tbsp olive oil
1 onion, finely chopped
2-3 cloves garlic, crushed
1 bay leaf
a large pinch of dried Provençal herbs
4 large ripe tomatoes (preferably Marmande), peeled, deseeded and chopped
salt and freshly ground black pepper
50 g/2 oz black olives, stoned and chopped

*1.* First make the Provençal sauce: combine the oil, onion, garlic, herbs and tomatoes in a bowl. Season, cover and cook on HIGH for 5 minutes, stirring halfway through. Stir in the chopped olives and set aside.
*2.* Cut off the bacon rinds and lay the rashers on a roasting rack or a double thickness of kitchen paper. Cover with another double thickness of paper and cook on HIGH for 30 seconds per rasher, or until well cooked. It will become crisper during the standing time. Remove the top layers of paper and leave the bacon to stand while you cook the mussels.
*3.* Put half the mussels and the wine in a casserole, cover and cook on HIGH for 5 minutes, shaking the casserole occasionally and stirring halfway through. Discard any mussels which have not opened. Using a slotted spoon, transfer the others to a heatproof serving dish, leaving the cooking liquid in the casserole.
*4.* Put the remaining mussels into the casserole, cover and cook as before. Transfer the mussels to the serving dish and sprinkle with parsley.

*5.* Crumble the bacon over the mussels. Discard the bay leaf from the Provençal sauce and pour the sauce over the mussels. Sprinkle with Parmesan cheese and cook on HIGH for 2 minutes to heat through. Garnish with more chopped parsley and serve piping hot.

# MONKFISH KEBABS

*Monkfish has a sweet, nutty flavour and a firm texture, making it perfect for kebabs. Serve on a bed of rice with a colourful Provençal sauce.*

SERVES 4

700 g/1 ½ lb monkfish tail, skinned
8 rashers of unsmoked streaky bacon, rinds removed
8 pickling onions, peeled, or 2 small onions, peeled and quartered
1 green pepper, deseeded and cut into chunks
8 cherry tomatoes
1 tsp olive oil
2 tbsp soy sauce
1 tsp lemon juice
1-2 cloves garlic, crushed
Provençal sauce, to serve (see p. 23)

*1.* Cut off the monkfish from the bone, then cut each fillet into 12 equal-sized chunks.
*2.* Stretch the bacon rashers with the flat side of a knife and cut each horizontally into 3 pieces. Wrap the chunks of monkfish in the bacon and thread them on to 4 long or 8 short wooden skewers, alternating them with onions, chunks of pepper and tomatoes. Arrange the kebabs on a roasting rack or in a flat dish.
*3.* Mix together the olive oil, soy sauce, lemon juice and garlic and brush half over the kebabs. Cover and cook on HIGH for 4 minutes.
*4.* Turn the kebabs and rearrange them on the rack or dish. Brush with the remaining soy sauce mixture, cover again and cook on HIGH for another 4 minutes, until the monkfish is firm. Serve with Provençal sauce, stirring the cooking juices from the fish and bacon into the sauce.

Moules Provençales

# PERCH À LA BOURGUIGNONNE

*Freshwater perch is often caught by coarse fishermen, but I recently discovered ocean perch in my local supermarket. Its robust texture goes well with this red wine sauce. Ocean perch has an attractive reddish skin. If you want to leave it on when you serve the fish, be sure to scrape off the scales before cooking, as they are rather large and unpalatable.*

SERVES 4

4 ocean perch fillets, about 450 g/1 lb
2 tbsp Court bouillon (see p. 20)
1 tbsp olive oil
12 button onions, (frozen will do)
4 fresh sage leaves
100 ml/3 ½ fl oz red wine
1 tsp butter, softened
1 tsp plain flour
salt and freshly ground black pepper
1 tbsp chopped fresh parsley or a few fresh sage leaves, to garnish

*1.* Scrape off the scales from the skin of the perch. Lay the fillets in a shallow dish, skin side up, pour over the court bouillon, cover and cook on HIGH for 4 minutes. Leave the perch in the court bouillon while you make the sauce.
*2.* Put the oil and onions into a bowl and cook on HIGH for 3-4 minutes, until the onions are almost soft, stirring halfway through. Add the sage and wine and pour in the cooking liquid from the perch. Cover and cook on HIGH for 2 minutes.
*3.* Blend the butter and flour to a paste and stir it into the sauce, a little at a time. Cover and cook on HIGH for 2-3 minutes, until the sauce has thickened, stirring after 1 minute. Season to taste with salt and freshly ground black pepper.
*4.* Peel off the fish skin if you like (I prefer to leave it on), and pour the sauce and onions over the perch. Sprinkle with chopped parsley or garnish with a few sage leaves (not too many, as the flavour is very strong).

# GENOESE SARDINES

*Although Italy is normally associated with pasta, Genoa is famous for its potato-based dishes. This simple and delicious recipe is typical of the region and is equally good made with mackerel fillets or other oily fish.*

SERVES 4

700 g/1 ½ lb potatoes, very thinly sliced
175 ml/6 fl oz olive oil
2-3 cloves garlic, finely chopped
50 g/2 oz chopped fresh parsley (flat-leaved, if possible)
salt and freshly ground black pepper
12 large fresh sardines, cleaned and heads removed
*Garnish*
chopped fresh parsley
1 tsp grated lemon zest

*1.* Arrange the sliced potatoes in a large shallow dish. Whisk together the oil, garlic and chopped parsley, season to taste with salt and pepper and pour half the mixture over the potatoes. Cover and cook on HIGH for about 5 minutes, until the potatoes are half cooked.
*2.* Lay the sardines on top of the potatoes, alternating them head to tail, and pour over the remaining oil mixture. Cover and cook on HIGH for 8-10 minutes, until the potatoes and sardines are tender.
*3.* Sprinkle with chopped parsley and grated lemon zest and serve hot.

# HERB PASTA WITH SMOKED TROUT

*Any dried pasta shapes can be used for this filling dish, and it is equally good made with other cooked smoked fish, such as eel or finnan haddie. If you can't find herb pasta, add a few extra fresh herbs to the sauce.*

SERVES 4

350 g/12 oz herb pasta shapes
2 litres/3½ pints boiling water
salt
225 g/8 oz tiny broccoli florets
4 small or 2 medium courgettes, very thinly sliced
2 tbsp olive oil
450 g/1 lb smoked trout fillets
225 ml/8 fl oz Greek-style yogurt
freshly ground black pepper
finely chopped mixed fresh herbs, such as parsley, chives, basil or tarragon, to garnish

*1.* Put the pasta shapes into a large bowl, pour on the boiling water and add salt to taste. Cover and cook on HIGH for about 8 minutes, until just *al dente*. Do not drain the pasta, but run in a little cold water to prevent further cooking, then leave to stand while you make the sauce.
*2.* Combine the broccoli florets, courgettes and oil in a bowl, cover and cook on HIGH for 3-4 minutes, stirring halfway through, until the vegetables are crisp.
*3.* To make the sauce, discard the trout skin and flake the flesh into a bowl, then stir in the yogurt and season to taste with salt and freshly ground black pepper. Cover and cook on HIGH for 2-3 minutes, until slightly thickened.
*4.* Drain the pasta and put it back into the large bowl. Stir in the vegetables, pour over the sauce and toss gently. Sprinkle over the fresh herbs and serve at once.

# MONKFISH MEDALLIONS WITH RATATOUILLE

*The hearty flavour of ratatouille suits monkfish surprisingly well. Add as much garlic as you like or dare! If really ripe, tasty tomatoes are in season, skin and chop 4 or 6 and use them instead of the canned tomatoes.*

SERVES 4

450 g/1 lb monkfish fillet
4 tbsp olive oil
2-3 cloves garlic, crushed
1 small aubergine
salt
4 small courgettes
1 onion, sliced
½ red pepper, deseeded and sliced
½ green pepper, deseeded and sliced
400 g/14 oz can chopped tomatoes
1 bay leaf
1 sprig thyme
freshly ground black pepper

*1.* Place the monkfish on a plate. Mix together 1 tbsp olive oil and 1 garlic clove and brush all over the monkfish. Cover and leave in a cool place for 1 hour.
*2.* Meanwhile, slice the aubergine and sprinkle both sides of each slice with salt. Place in a colander, put a weighted plate on top and leave for about 45 minutes to draw out the bitter juices.
*3.* To make the ratatouille, rinse the aubergine slices thoroughly to get rid of all the salt, pat dry and cut into 1-cm/½-in chunks. Top and tail the courgettes and cut into 1-cm/½-in slices.
*4.* Heat the remaining olive oil in a large covered casserole on HIGH for 1 minute. Add the aubergine chunks, stir well to coat them in oil, then cook on HIGH for 3 minutes, or until tender, stirring halfway through.
*5.* Add the onion and the remaining garlic, stir and cook on HIGH for 3 minutes, until the onion begins to soften. Add the red and green peppers, stir and cook for another 2 minutes.
*6.* Add the courgettes, stir well, cover and cook on HIGH for 2 more minutes, then add the

tomatoes with their juice, the bay leaf and thyme. Season to taste with salt and pepper, cover and cook for 3-5 minutes, or until the vegetables are soft but not mushy, stirring after 2 minutes. Remove the bay leaf and thyme.

7. Cut the monkfish into 2-cm/¾-in slices and lay them down the centre of the ratatouille, embedding them slightly in the vegetables. Season, cover the casserole and cook on HIGH for 4 minutes, turning the medallions over halfway through. They should be just cooked. Leave to stand for 5 minutes before serving.

# SKATE WITH BLACK BUTTER AND CAPERS

*Unlike most other fish, skate tastes better when it is 2 or 3 days old. Once the wings are cooked, the flesh slides easily off the bones. Use unsalted butter for the black butter; salted butter may burn as it becomes hot.*

### SERVES 2

2 skate wings, about 350 g/12 oz each
2 tbsp red wine vinegar
75 g/3 oz unsalted butter
2 tbsp small capers
sea salt and freshly ground black pepper
1 tbsp finely chopped fresh parsley

1. Put the skate wings into a shallow dish with half the vinegar and 100 ml/3½ fl oz water. Cover and cook on HIGH for 7-8 minutes until tender. Drain and leave to stand.

2. Put the butter into a medium bowl, cover and cook on HIGH for 5-6 minutes until it turns nutty brown. Do not let it burn, or it will taste very nasty. Stir in the remaining vinegar and the capers, cover and cook on HIGH for 1 minute.

3. Drain the skate, season with sea salt and pepper and sprinkle with parsley. Pour over the black butter and serve at once.

*Left:* Skate with Black Butter and Capers
*Right:* Monkfish Medallions with Ratatouille
(page 89)

# CRISPY COD IN MUSTARD SAUCE

*The mild flavour of French mustard is very good with most white fish. If you don't like potato crisps, use brown breadcrumbs instead.*

SERVES 4

450 g/1 lb cod or other white fish steaks
1 bayleaf
½ onion, sliced
2 parsley stalks
3 tbsp white wine or Fish stock (see p. 20)
*Sauce*
50 g/2 oz butter
2 tbsp plain flour
150 ml/5 fl oz milk
150 ml/5 fl oz single cream
2 tbsp French mustard
salt and freshly ground pepper
*Topping*
15 g/½ oz butter
1 tbsp French mustard
3 tbsp potato crisps, finely crushed
1 tbsp finely chopped fresh parsley

*1.* Put the fish in a shallow dish with the bay leaf, onion and parsley, pour over the wine or stock, cover and cook on HIGH for 4-5 minutes, until tender. Leave to stand while you make the sauce.
*2.* Put the butter in a bowl and melt on HIGH for 45-60 seconds. Whisk in the flour and cook on HIGH for 1 minute to make a roux.
*3.* Combine the milk, cream and mustard in a jug and heat on HIGH for about 1½ minutes, until hot but not boiling. Gradually whisk the hot mixture into the roux, then cook on HIGH for 3-4 minutes until the sauce is thick and smooth, stirring every minute. Strain the cooking liquor from the fish into the sauce, stir well and season.
*4.* Flake the fish, discarding any skin and bones and stir it into the sauce. Put into a serving dish.
*5.* To make the topping, melt the butter on HIGH for 30 seconds, stir in the mustard, crushed crisps and parsley and sprinkle the topping evenly over the fish. Cook on HIGH for 1½-2 minutes, until heated  through.

# TROUT FILLETS AU GRATIN

*Ready-filleted pink trout are available at many supermarkets. The fillets tend to be quite large, so allow one per person. Fillets of halibut are also delicious prepared this way.*

SERVES 4

100 g/4 oz button mushrooms, thinly sliced
25 g/1 oz butter
4 pink trout fillets, about 700 g/1 ½ lb
salt and freshly ground black pepper
50 ml/2 fl oz dry white wine
juice of ½ lemon
50 ml/2 fl oz double cream
freshly grated nutmeg
2 tbsp home-made dried breadcrumbs
1-2 tbsp finely chopped fresh parsley

*1.* Put the mushrooms and butter into a shallow, heatproof dish. Lay the trout fillets on top, season and pour over the wine and lemon juice. Cover and cook on HIGH for 4-5 minutes; the trout should still be slightly opaque in the centre.
*2.* Strain the cooking liquid into a jug and leave the fish to rest, covered.
*3.* Stir the cream and a pinch of nutmeg into the cooking liquid and cook on HIGH for 3-4 minutes until it boils and thickens.
*4.* Pour the sauce over the trout fillets, sprinkle over the breadcrumbs in an even layer and place under a hot grill until browned. Scatter over the parsley and serve.

# TUNA STEAKS NIÇOISE

*Since fresh tuna has a firm, meaty texture and needs longer cooking than most fish, it is ideal for braising in a robust sauce. As it is very rich, you may find that two steaks will be enough to serve four people.*

SERVES 2-4

2 fresh tuna steaks, about 225 g/8 oz each
salt and freshly ground black pepper
1 tsp lemon juice
½ tsp dried Provençal herbs
50 g/2 oz can anchovies in oil
1 onion, thinly sliced
2 cloves garlic, finely chopped
1 red and 1 yellow pepper, deseeded, cored and cut into thin strips
400 g/14 oz can chopped tomatoes
1 tbsp capers
50 g/2 oz small black olives
chopped fresh parsley, to garnish

*1.* Heat a browning dish on HIGH for 5-8 minutes, or according to the manufacturer's instructions.
*2.* Season the tuna steaks with salt, pepper and lemon juice and sprinkle the herbs over both sides of the fish. Drain the oil from the anchovies and reserve it. Coarsely chop the anchovies and set aside.
*3.* When the browning dish is hot, put in the oil, onion and garlic and cook on HIGH for 2 minutes to soften the onion. Stir in the pepper strips and cook on HIGH for 2 minutes, stirring after 1 minute.
*4.* Push the vegetables to the edge of the dish and put in the tuna steaks. Cook on HIGH for 3 minutes to seal one side, then turn the steaks over and cook for another 3 minutes.
*5.* Mix together the tomatoes and capers and pour them over the tuna. Scatter the chopped anchovies over the top, then cook on HIGH for 10-12 minutes, until the tuna is tender.
*6.* Scatter in the olives and cook on HIGH for about 1 minute to heat them. Transfer the tuna to a serving dish, spoon over the sauce and olives and sprinkle with parsley before serving.

# FILLETS OF BRILL WITH PICKLES

*A tasty recipe to spice up the sometimes bland flavour of brill.*

SERVES 4

450 g/1 lb brill fillets
2 tbsp olive oil
1 tbsp red wine vinegar
1 large dill pickle or pickled gherkin, finely chopped
6 pimento-stuffed olives, finely chopped
2 tsp capers, finely chopped
1 tsp finely chopped fresh dill
salt and freshly ground black pepper
*Garnish*
sprigs of dill
lemon twists

*1.* Lay the brill fillets in a shallow dish, skin side up. Mix together all the ingredients except the garnish and spread the mixture thickly and evenly over the fish.
*2.* Cover and cook on HIGH for about 5 minutes, until the brill is tender. Decorate with sprigs of dill and lemon twists and serve immediately, or, if you wish, quickly brown the fish under a hot grill before serving.

# SEAFOOD TURBANE

*This attractive turbane looks spectacular with colourful Provençal sauce spooned into the centre of the ring. Use any flat fish fillets to line the mould.*

### SERVES 6

25 g/1 oz butter, plus 1 tsp for greasing the mould
4 small leeks, outer leaves reserved and remainder
very finely shredded
4 double plaice fillets, skinned
100 g/4 oz Gruyère cheese, grated
grated zest of ½ lemon
25 g/1 oz fresh white breadcrumbs
2 tbsp finely chopped fresh chervil
2 eggs, lightly beaten
150 ml/5 fl oz single cream
salt and freshly ground black pepper
100 g/4 oz cooked peeled prawns
Provençal sauce, to serve (optional, see p. 23)
sprigs of chervil, to garnish

*1.* Grease a 20 cm/8 in ring mould with the 1 tsp butter. Wash the reserved leek leaves and use them to line the mould at regular intervals, leaving gaps in between to give a striped effect.
*2.* Line the mould with the plaice fillets, with the skin side uppermost, arranging them inside the leek leaves where necessary.
*3.* Put the butter and shredded leeks into a bowl, cover and cook on HIGH for 3-5 minutes to soften the leeks. Stir in the Gruyère cheese, lemon zest, breadcrumbs, chervil, eggs and cream. Cover and cook on MEDIUM for 5 minutes, until thickened. Season to taste with salt and pepper.
*4.* Spoon half the mixture into the mould. Lay the prawns in an even layer on top, then cover with the remaining leek mixture and press down gently. Fold over the overlapping plaice fillets and leek leaves, cover and cook on HIGH for 5-7 minutes, or until the filling is just firm.
*5.* Place a wire rack over the mould. Invert the rack and mould on to a baking tray to catch the liquid and leave to drain for about 5 minutes.

Seafood Turbane

Meanwhile, heat the sauce, if necessary.
*6.* Turn over the mould and rack, remove the rack and unmould the turbane on to a serving dish. Using a serrated knife, carefully cut into slices and arrange 2 or 3 on each plate garnished with a sprig of chervil, or fill the centre of the turbane with hot sauce and serve the rest of the sauce separately.

# WHITING WITH MUSHROOMS

*Whiting is not a very popular fish, probably because of its greyish flesh and ugly face. It is certainly true that old, stale whiting is an unattractive proposition, but really fresh whiting is cheap and tasty. Choose fish with bright eyes and shiny skin and you will be surprised how good they taste.*

### SERVES 4

100 g/4 oz butter
2 small onions, finely chopped
175 g/6 oz button mushrooms, coarsely chopped
100 ml/3 ½ fl oz dry white wine
salt and freshly ground black pepper
4 whiting, about 300 g/11 oz each, filleted
1 tbsp lemon juice
1 tbsp chopped fresh parsley

*1.* Put the butter and onions into a bowl and cook on HIGH for 4-5 minutes, until the onions are soft and golden brown.
*2.* Stir in the mushrooms and cook on HIGH for 2 minutes to soften them. Stir in the wine and season to taste with salt and pepper.
*3.* Arrange the whiting fillets head to tail and skin side down in a shallow dish. If they are very long, fold the tail ends under so that the fillets fit the dish.
*4.* Spoon over the mushroom mixture, cover and cook on HIGH for 5-7 minutes, until the fish is tender. Sprinkle with lemon juice and parsley, leave to stand for 5 minutes, then serve.

# KOULIBIAC

*This delicious Russian fish pie is best served hot, but also makes an excellent picnic dish when cold. If you don't have a combination oven, bake the finished pie in a conventional oven.*

SERVES 6

100 g/4 oz long grain rice
300 ml/½ pint boiling water
salt
450 g/1 lb salmon fillet
50 ml/2 fl oz Court bouillon (see p. 20) or dry white
wine
25 g/1 oz butter, plus extra for greasing
1 onion, finely chopped
100 g/4 oz button mushrooms, finely sliced
2 eggs
2 tbsp finely chopped fresh parsley
1 tsp lemon juice
freshly ground black pepper
450 g/1 lb puff pastry
1 egg beaten with 1 tsp milk, to glaze

*1.* Put the rice into a casserole with the boiling water and ½ tsp salt, cover and cook on HIGH for 5-7 minutes, until the rice is just tender. Leave to stand while you cook the salmon.

*2.* Put the salmon into a dish with the court bouillon or wine, cover and cook on HIGH for 3-4 minutes, until just tender. Set aside.

*3.* Melt 25 g/1 oz butter in a bowl on HIGH for about 1 minute. Stir in the onion and cook on HIGH for 3 minutes, until the onion is soft. Add the mushrooms and cook them for another 1-2 minutes. Leave to cool.

*4.* Break the eggs into a ramekin, pierce the yolks with a cocktail stick, cover and cook on HIGH for 2-2½ minutes. Leave to stand until the yolks are hard, then chop the eggs.

*5.* Skin the salmon and remove any bones, then flake the flesh into fairly large pieces. Stir the cooled mushroom mixture into the cooked rice, add the parsley, then carefully fold in the chopped eggs and flaked salmon. Season the mixture with lemon juice, salt and pepper to taste.

*6.* Roll out the pastry into a long rectangle, about 30 × 20 cm/12 × 8 in. Cut the rectangle in half to give you two 15 × 20 cm/6 × 8 in rectangles. Place one rectangle on a buttered baking tray and pile on the salmon and rice mixture, shaping it with your hands and leaving a 2 cm/¾ in border. Brush the border with egg glaze, then top with the other piece of pastry. Pinch the edges together and knock up.

*7.* Use the pastry trimmings to make decorations (leaves or little fish) and attach them to the koulibiac with egg glaze. Refrigerate for 20 minutes.

*8.* Brush the top of the koulibiac with a little egg glaze and bake on COMBINATION 2 for 20-25 minutes, until the pastry is risen and golden. Alternatively, bake in a preheated conventional oven at 230°C/450°F/Gas Mark 8 for about 25 minutes until golden brown.

# PLAICE EN SURPRISE

*If you can find small whole plaice, allow one per person; a larger fish will serve two. It is best to cook large plaice separately, leaving one to rest while the other is cooking.*

SERVES 2-4

2 whole plaice, about 350 g/12 oz each, cleaned and black skin removed
1 onion, finely chopped
2 cloves garlic, finely chopped
75 g/3 oz fresh brown breadcrumbs
2 tbsp olive oil
100 g/4 oz very white button mushrooms, finely chopped
2 tomatoes, peeled, deseeded and finely diced
1 tsp fresh marjoram or ½ tsp dried mixed herbs
1 tbsp finely chopped fresh parsley
1 tbsp lemon juice
1-2 tsp grated lemon zest
salt and freshly ground black pepper
*Garnish*
8-10 cherry tomatoes
8-10 small button mushrooms, stalks removed
6 sprigs parsley

*1.* Trim off the fins and tails from the plaice and lay the fish white side upwards. Using a very sharp, supple knife, make an incision down the backbone of each fish. Insert the flat of the knife into the incision and cut the flesh away from the bone with a stroking motion to make a pocket on either side.
*2.* Combine the onion, garlic, breadcrumbs and half the oil in a shallow dish and cook on COMBINATION 5 for 6-8 minutes, until the crumbs are crisp, stirring halfway through, or microwave on HIGH for 2-3 minutes. Stir in the mushrooms, tomatoes, herbs and lemon juice and zest and cook on HIGH for 2 minutes, until the mushrooms are just cooked. Taste and season as necessary.
*3.* Stuff the pockets in the plaice with the filling, brush the fish with olive oil and place in the grill pan on a high rack. Prick the skin of the tomatoes and brush them and the mushroom caps with oil. Arrange them around the fish and cook on COMBINATION 5 for 6-8 minutes, until the plaice is cooked through and lightly browned. Alternatively, cover and microwave on HIGH for 5-7 minues then brown under a preheated medium hot grill.
*4.* Arrange the tomatoes and mushrooms decoratively at the head and tail of the fish and garnish with parsley sprigs.

# SICILIAN SWORDFISH

*Swordfish has a firm, meaty texture which benefits from a sharp sauce and longer cooking than most fish. This Sicilian sauce perfectly balances the rich flavour of the fish.*

SERVES 4

1 tsp salt
2 tbsp lemon juice
1 tsp dried oregano
4 tbsp olive oil
freshly ground black pepper
4 swordfish steaks, about 225 g/8 oz each
*Garnish*
lemon wedges
sprigs of fresh herbs

*1.* Whisk together the salt, lemon juice and oregano, then whisk in the olive oil, a little at a time and beat until the sauce is smooth and slightly thickened. Season with pepper.
*2.* Lay the swordfish steaks in a single layer in a shallow dish and pour over the sauce. Cover and cook on HIGH for 8-10 minutes, until very tender, basting the fish with the sauce from time to time.
*3.* Transfer the swordfish steaks to warmed serving plates and pour over the sauce. Leave to stand for 5 minutes then garnish with lemon wedges and fresh herbs and serve.

# Entertaining

I think fish is one of the nicest of all foods to serve to friends. It can be ultra elegant and luxurious, like Lobster Thermidor, or flamboyant and fun, like Paella. It takes very little time to cook these attractive main dishes, so you need not abandon your guests for long while you prepare their dinner.

Start the meal with a light first course which will not overwhelm the delicate fish which follows. One of the joys of fish is that it is light enough to allow you free rein with the pudding. You could hardly follow roast beef with a heavy chocolate creation, but after fish you can be as calorifically wild as you like.

## LOBSTER THERMIDOR

*It is better to use 1 large rather than 2 small lobsters for this extravagant dish, as it will contain a higher proportion of edible flesh and the meat will be sweeter. Lobster is so expensive that this recipe caters only for dining à deux.*

### SERVES 2

700 g/1½ lb boiled lobster or 2 lobsters, about
450 g/1 lb each
25 g/1 oz butter
50 g/2 oz shallots, finely chopped
100 g/4 oz button mushrooms, finely sliced
1 tbsp plain flour
a pinch of paprika
salt and freshly ground black pepper
50 ml/2 fl oz hot Fish stock (see p. 20)
100 ml/3 ½ fl oz double cream
1 tsp Dijon mustard
2 egg yolks, beaten
2-3 tbsp dry sherry
3 tbsp freshly grated Parmesan cheese

*1.* Halve the lobster lengthways and crack the claws. Extract all the meat (you may need a lobster pick) and cut into large dice. Keep the shells for later.
*2.* Put the butter and shallots into a large bowl and cook on HIGH for 2-3 minutes, until the shallots are soft. Add the mushrooms and cook on HIGH for 2 minutes, until just tender, stirring after 1 minute.
*3.* Stir in the flour and paprika and a little salt and pepper and cook on HIGH for 1-2 minutes. Stir in the hot stock, cream and mustard and blend until very smooth. Cook on MEDIUM for 4-5 minutes, until the sauce has thickened, stirring halfway through.
*4.* Pour 4 tbsp of hot sauce into the egg yolks, stir well, then stir this mixture back into the sauce. Add the sherry and season to taste. Cover and cook on MEDIUM for 3-4 minutes, until the sauce is thick and smooth.
*5.* Stir the diced lobster into the sauce, cover and cook on HIGH for 1-2 minutes, until hot. Divide the mixture between the 2 halves of the shell. Sprinkle the top with Parmesan cheese and cook on a high rack on COMBINATION 5 for 5 minutes, until browned, or brown under a preheated hot grill. Serve at once.

Lobster Thermidor

# SOLE VÉRONIQUE

*This delectable dish adapts itself perfectly to microwave cooking. The sole fillets remain perfectly moist and the grapes retain all their succulence. It really is worth using Dover sole; buy 2 whole sole and have them filleted, then you can use the bones and trimmings for stock. If seedless grapes are not available, substitute peeled and halved Italian Muscat-type grapes.*

SERVES 4

8 Dover sole fillets, about 75 g/3 oz each, skinned
50 g/2 oz butter
2 shallots, finely chopped
200 ml/7 fl oz dry white wine
2 egg yolks, lightly beaten
4 tbsp double cream
salt and freshly ground white pepper
225 g/8 oz small seedless white grapes, peeled
a tiny bunch of grapes, to garnish (optional)

*1.* Roll up the sole fillets, skinned side inwards, and secure with a wooden cocktail stick.
*2.* Put half the butter and the shallots into a shallow dish and cook on HIGH for 2 minutes. Pour in the wine and cook on HIGH for 2 more minutes, until the shallots are very soft.
*3.* Arrange the rolled sole fillets in a single layer on top of the shallots, cover and cook on HIGH for 4-6 minutes, until the sole is just tender.
*4.* Arrange the sole fillets on a warmed serving dish, carefully remove the cocktail sticks and keep the sole warm while you make the sauce.
*5.* Cook the cooking liquid on HIGH for about 5 minutes, until slightly reduced, then stir in the egg yolks, cream and the remaining butter. Whisk well, then cook on MEDIUM for 2-3 minutes, until slightly thickened, stirring every minute. Do not let the sauce boil or it will curdle. Season to taste with salt and pepper.
*6.* Add the peeled grapes and cook on MEDIUM for 1 minute, until heated through. Pour the sauce and grapes over the sole, top with a tiny bunch of grapes, if you like, and serve immediately. Alternatively, brown the top lightly under a preheated grill before garnishing and serving.

# PAELLA

*This must be one of the all-time favourites for a party. You can vary the ingredients as you like, but do include some chorizo sausage for an authentic Spanish flavour.*

SERVES 6-8

50 ml/2 fl oz olive oil
1 onion, finely sliced
3-4 cloves garlic, finely chopped
350 g/12 oz boneless chicken or rabbit, cut into chunks
225 g/8 oz squid, cleaned and cut into rings
450 g/1 lb long grain or risotto rice
1 red pepper, deseeded and cut into chunks
a large pinch of saffron threads
1 litre/1 ¾ pints boiling Fish stock (see p. 20)
400 g/14 oz can tomatoes, drained and chopped
225 g/8 oz chorizo sausage, cut into 1 cm/½ in slices
6 cooked crab claws or langoustines
a pinch of cayenne pepper
salt and freshly ground black pepper
450 g/1 lb mussels or clams, scrubbed

*1.* Put the oil, onion and garlic into a large casserole and cook on HIGH for 2-3 minutes, until the onion begins to soften.
*2.* Add the chicken or rabbit and squid, stir to coat in the oil, cover and cook on HIGH for 4-6 minutes, until tender. Remove the chicken and squid with a slotted spoon and set aside.
*3.* Put the rice, red pepper and saffron into the oil left in the casserole and stir until the rice is well coated with oil. Pour in the boiling stock, cover the casserole and cook on HIGH for 10-12 minutes, until the rice is almost done.
*4.* Stir in the chicken, squid, tomatoes, chorizo and the crab claws or langoustines, re-cover and cook on HIGH for 3-5 minutes, until all the liquid has been absorbed and the rice is tender. Season with cayenne, salt and pepper and mix carefully.
*5.* Lay the mussels or clams decoratively on top of the paella, cover and cook on HIGH for 3-4 minutes, until all the shellfish have opened. Discard any which have not. Serve very hot.

# POISSON EN CROÛTE

*The great joy of this dish is that it looks spectacular and is so versatile. You can use almost any kind of large, firm fish, from sea bass (my own favourite) to salmon, cod or grey mullet. Let your imagination run riot with the pastry crust, which can be a simple rectangle or a highly decorated fish shape, and can be cooked either in a combination or conventional oven.*

### SERVES 8

1.25 kg/2 ½ lb sea bass or grey mullet, cleaned, skinned and filleted
4 parsley stalks
2 bay leaves
50 ml/2 fl oz dry white wine
salt and freshly ground pepper
100 g/4 oz watercress leaves
4 sprigs tarragon
50 g/2 oz butter
700 g/1½ lb puff pastry, thawed if frozen
1 tsp fine semolina
beaten egg, to glaze the pastry
sprigs of watercress, to garnish
Herb and yogurt sauce (see p. 21) or Lemon butter sauce (see p. 23), to serve

*1.* Place the fish fillets in a shallow dish with the parsley stalks and bay leaves. Pour over the wine, cover and cook on HIGH for about 3 minutes, until opaque. Season with salt and pepper, then strain the cooking liquid into a bowl and leave the fish to cool.

*2.* Heat the strained cooking liquid on HIGH for 3 minutes, until boiling. Add the watercress leaves and tarragon and cook on HIGH for 30 seconds. Drain well and finely chop the blanched watercress and tarragon. Mix in the butter and season to taste.

*3.* On a lightly floured surface, roll out one third of the pastry to a rectangle or fish shape 2.5 cm/ 1 in larger all round than the fish. Sprinkle over a fine film of semolina; this will prevent the pastry from going soggy during baking. Lay one fillet on the pastry and spread over the chopped watercress mixture. Cover with the other fillet.

*4.* Roll out another one third of the pastry to a slightly larger rectangle or fish shape and use it to cover the fish. Brush the edges of the pastry with beaten egg and seal.

*5.* Roll out the remaining pastry and cut into 'scales', shell shapes or whatever takes your creative fancy. Stick the shapes on to the pastry-wrapped fish with beaten egg, then carefully transfer to a dish and refrigerate for 30 minutes.

*6.* Carefully brush the pastry with beaten egg and cook on COMBINATION 2 for 25-30 minutes, until the pastry is risen and golden, or bake in a conventional oven preheated to 230°C/450°F/Gas Mark 8 for about 30 minutes. Garnish with watercress sprigs and serve with the sauce.

# WHOLE POACHED SALMON

*One of the nicest of all party dishes is a whole salmon, resplendently displayed on a platter. Most microwave ovens, though, are simply not large enough to take a whole fish, so why not cut up your salmon, cook it, then restore it to its original glory? You will be amazed at how easy it is to hide the joins artistically. If you bone the fish before reassembling it, it will be much easier to serve.*

### SERVES 16-20

3-3.5 kg/7-8 lb salmon, gutted
100 ml/3 ½ fl oz Fish stock or Court bouillon (see p. 20) or dry white wine
4 parsley stalks
2 sprigs tarragon
½ lemon, cut into slices
300 ml/½ pint Mayonnaise (see p. 25)
1 cucumber
*Garnish*
lime slices
sprigs of fresh herbs and watercress

*1.* Cut off the salmon head just below the gills, wash it in cold water and pat dry. Cut off the tail end about 20 cm/8 in from the tail. If the central part of the body is still too large for your microwave oven, cut it in half.

2. Weigh all the salmon pieces. Put the head into a shallow dish, pour over half the stock, court bouillon or wine, cover and cook on HIGH for 5 minutes per 450 g/1 lb. Remove the cooked head from the dish (it may still look slightly under-cooked, but don't worry; it will continue to cook as it stands).

3. Arrange the salmon head at the top of a serving platter or long foil-lined tray. Cover loosely with foil.

4. Put 3 parsley stalks, a sprig of tarragon and half the lemon slices inside the largest piece of salmon, place in the poaching liquid, adding a little more stock if necessary, cover and cook on HIGH, allowing 4 minutes per 450 g/1 lb. Remove it from the dish, cover with foil and leave to rest.

5. Stuff the tail piece with the remaining parsley sprig, tarragon and lemon, place in the dish, cover and cook on HIGH for 3½-4 minutes per 450 g/1 lb (the tail needs less cooking time than the body as it is thinner).

6. As each cooked piece of salmon becomes cool enough to handle, carefully peel off the skin and scrape off any greyish flesh. Using a fish slice, lift the top layer of fish from the bone, remove the backbone and any smaller stray bones, then replace the top layer on the bottom layer.

7. On your serving platter, reassemble the cold salmon into its original shape, sandwiching the pieces together with the mayonnaise. Slice the cucumber very finely (a food processor is best for this) and cover the salmon with overlapping slices to look like scales.

8. If you like, put any remaining mayonnaise into a piping bag with a 1 cm/½ in nozzle and pipe decorative rosettes of mayonnaise over the joins in the fish. Arrange sprigs of herbs over the rosettes and garnish with lime slices and watercress.

Whole Poached Salmon (page 101)

# PRINCE OF WALES SALMON

*This delectable dinner party dish can be served hot or cold and is wonderful for a grand picnic. It can also be made using a whole filleted salmon trout. Ask the fishmonger for the salmon skin and bones to make the stock.*

SERVES 6

1 kg/2 ¼ lb salmon tail piece, filleted and skinned
50 g/2 oz wholegrain mustard
skin and bones from the salmon
700 g/1 ½ lb leeks, finely sliced
75 g/3 oz butter
salt and freshly ground white pepper
4 sprigs tarragon
1 tbsp dry white wine

*1.* Spread the insides of the salmon fillets with wholegrain mustard, cover and place in the fridge while you prepare the stock and leek purée.
*2.* Put the salmon skin and bones into a casserole, pour in 350 ml/12 fl oz water, cover and cook on HIGH for 5 minutes, then on MEDIUM for 15 minutes to make a delicious stock.
*3.* Put the sliced leeks into a casserole, strain the stock over, cover and cook on HIGH for 5-7 minutes, until the leeks are just soft but still look fresh and green. Drain and reserve the cooking stock.
*4.* Put the leeks and butter in a blender or food processor, purée until smooth, then season to taste with salt and pepper. Spread half the purée over the insides of the salmon fillets and sandwich them together, so that the leek purée forms a filling.
*5.* Lay the salmon on a sheet of microwave-safe clingfilm large enough to enclose the salmon completely, top with the sprigs of tarragon and sprinkle with wine. Fold over the edges of the clingfilm and seal tightly. Cook on HIGH for 8-10 minutes (lift up the top layer and peek inside to check the cooking; the flesh should still be rosy and slightly opaque), then leave to stand for 5 minutes while you make the sauce.
*6.* Mix the remaining leek purée with the reserved stock to make a sauce, pour into a sauceboat and cook on HIGH until just hot. Slice the fish vertically to reveal the pretty pink and green layers and serve the sauce separately.

# PROVENÇAL AÏOLI

*I think this is one of the very finest of all dishes to share with friends. Nothing can beat the sight of a huge platter piled with crisp, colourful vegetables and salt cod, with its accompanying bowl of golden, garlicky aioli sauce. This aioli is a meal in itself; serve only crusty French bread and perhaps some fresh fruit afterwards. Vary the vegetables according to what is in season and serve them raw or cooked to crisp perfection.*

SERVES 6

1 kg/2 ¼ lb salt cod
bouquet garni
12 new potatoes, unpeeled and scrubbed
salt
12 small carrots, scrubbed
a pinch of sugar
225 g/8 oz French beans, topped and tailed
225 g/8 oz broccoli or cauliflower florets
6 hard-boiled eggs
1 red pepper, cut into strips
2 fennel bulbs, cut into strips
6 cooked unpeeled prawns or langoustines, to garnish (optional)
600 ml/1 pint Aïoli, to serve (see p. 25)

*1.* Soak the salt cod overnight in cold water, rinse thoroughly to remove excess salt and drain. Put the cod into a shallow dish with 150 ml/5 fl oz water and the bouquet garni. Cover and cook on HIGH for 3-5 minutes, until the water is boiling.
*2.* Reduce the power to MEDIUM and cook for 8-10 minutes, until the cod flakes away from the bone. Leave it in the cooking liquid and set aside.
*3.* Place the potatoes into a bowl with 100 ml/ 3 ½ fl oz water and salt to taste, cover and cook on HIGH for about 8 minutes, or until just tender. Drain and set aside.

*4.* Put the carrots into a dish and add 100 ml/ 3 ½ fl oz water and a pinch of sugar, cover and cook on HIGH for about 5 minutes; they should still be very crunchy. Drain and set aside.

*5.* Cook the French beans with 4 tbsp water on HIGH for 3-4 minutes, until barely cooked. Refresh in cold water to preserve their fresh colour, then drain and set aside.

*6.* Cook the broccoli florets without added water on HIGH for 3 minutes, until bright green and very crisp. Refresh, then drain and set aside.

*7.* Strain the liquid from the cod and remove the skin. Break the flesh into large flakes. Shell the eggs and cut them into quarters. Pile the cod in the middle of an enormous platter and arrange the eggs and all the vegetables decoratively around the edge. Garnish with prawns or langoustines, if you like. Serve the aïoli in a large bowl, or give everyone an individual bowl. Be sure to provide fingerbowls and napkins!

# LETTUCE-WRAPPED SEA BASS WITH VEGETABLE MEDLEY

*Sea bass is a truly beautiful fish, both to look at and to eat. Unfortunately, it is extremely expensive – but sometimes a little extravagance is no bad thing! If the price is too daunting, use sea bream or grey mullet instead, but sea bass really is in a class of its own and makes a spectacularly simple dinner party dish.*

### SERVES 4

900 g/2 lb sea bass, scaled and cleaned
juice of ½ lemon
salt and freshly ground white pepper
6-8 large leaves from a round lettuce
2 celery stalks
4 small carrots
2 small turnips
1 small fennel bulb
100 g/4 oz butter
150 ml/5 fl oz dry white wine
100 ml/3 ½ fl oz double cream

*1.* Season the sea bass inside and out with lemon juice, salt and pepper.

*2.* Lay the lettuce leaves in a shallow dish, cover and cook on HIGH for 20-30 seconds to soften them. Refresh in iced water, drain and pat dry. If the leaves are very young and malleable, do not bother to blanch them.

*3.* Wrap the sea bass in the lettuce leaves so that it is completely enclosed. Set aside.

*4.* Cut the celery, carrots, turnips and fennel into thin batons. Put half the butter into a rectangular dish large enough to take the fish and cook on HIGH for 1-2 minutes, until melted. Add the vegetable batons, stir to coat with butter, cover and cook on HIGH for 3-5 minutes, until the vegetables are half cooked, stirring twice.

*5.* Spread the vegetables evenly over the bottom of the dish and carefully lay the fish on top. Pour over the wine, cover and cook on HIGH for about 8 minutes, until the bass is tender.

*6.* Using 2 fish slices, transfer the fish to a warmed serving dish. Lift the vegetables out of the poaching liquid with a slotted spoon and arrange them attractively around the fish. Keep warm while you make the sauce.

*7.* Pour the cooking liquid into a bowl and cook on HIGH for about 6 minutes, until reduced and slightly syrupy (it may be quicker to do this over conventional heat).

*8.* Meanwhile, dice the remaining butter. When the stock is ready, stir in the cream and cook on HIGH for 2 minutes, until boiling. Whisk in the diced butter, a piece at a time, until the sauce is smooth. Season to taste with salt and pepper, add a squeeze of lemon if necessary, then pour the sauce over the vegetables surrounding the bass and serve at once.

# Family Dishes

These inexpensive dishes are perfect for family meals and are attractive enough to persuade even non-fish eaters to give them a try. Children are often reluctant to eat fish because they have suffered greasy batter or bland, floury creations overcooked in tasteless sauce at school. There is no reason why fish pie, for example, should be like that; mine is colourful and full of flavour – perhaps it will convert them.

All these recipes are quick to prepare and make really substantial supper dishes. Make fresh fish part of your weekly meal plan; it takes no longer to cook than any ready-prepared food and it is much better for you.

## SPAGHETTI ALLE VONGOLE

*This spaghetti with clams is one of the most popular of all Italian dishes. Fresh clams are available all year round and provide plenty of messy eating entertainment.*

### SERVES 4-6

1 small onion, finely chopped
2 cloves garlic, finely chopped
50 ml/2 fl oz olive oil
400 g/14 oz can chopped tomatoes
1 tbsp tomato purée
150 ml/5 fl oz dry white wine
450 g/1 lb spaghetti
900 g/2 lb small fresh clams, scrubbed
2 tbsp finely chopped fresh parsley
1 tbsp chopped fresh basil or 1 tsp dried basil
salt and freshly ground black pepper

*1.* Put the onion, garlic and oil into a large bowl and cook on HIGH for 3 minutes, or until the onion is soft. Stir in the tomatoes, tomato purée and wine and cook on HIGH for 12-15 minutes, until the sauce is reduced and slightly thickened.

*2.* Meanwhile, cook the spaghetti conventionally in plenty of boiling salted water until *al dente*, then drain and keep warm in a colander set over a pan of simmering water.

*3.* Stir the clams into the tomato sauce, cover and cook on HIGH for 4-6 minutes, or until all the clams have opened, stirring every 2 minutes. Discard any clams which have not opened. Stir in the chopped parsley and basil and season the sauce with salt and pepper.

*4.* Mix in the spaghetti, grind over a little more pepper if you like and serve at once.

Spaghetti alle Vongole

# TUNA ROLL

*This unusual 'sausage' makes an excellent picnic or packed lunch dish. Serve it with Tartare sauce and some sweet cherry tomatoes.*

SERVES 6

100 g/4 oz potato
400 g/14 oz can tuna in oil
25 g/1 oz freshly grated Parmesan cheese
1-2 tbsp horseradish sauce
1 tbsp lemon juice
2 tbsp chopped fresh parsley
1 tbsp capers or finely chopped gherkins (optional)
1 egg
1 egg white
salt and freshly ground black pepper
300 ml/½ pint Court bouillon or Fish stock (see p. 20)
Tartare sauce, to serve (see p. 25)

*1.* Cut the potato into chunks, place in a bowl with 4 tbsp water, cover and cook on HIGH for 3-4 minutes, until soft. Mash it until very smooth.
*2.* Drain the tuna and put it into a blender or food processor with the Parmesan cheese, horseradish sauce, lemon juice, parsley and the capers or gherkins, if using. Process briefly until fairly smooth.
*3.* Add the egg and egg white and process until blended; the texture of the mixture should not be absolutely smooth. Stir in the mashed potato and season to taste with salt and pepper.
*4.* Spoon the mixture on to a sheet of microwave-safe clingfilm and shape into a 'sausage' about 7.5 cm/3 in in diameter. Roll it up tightly in the clingfilm and twist the ends tightly to secure them. Pierce the clingfilm all over in about 10 places with a needle so that the tuna roll can absorb the flavour of the court bouillon.
*5.* Lay the roll in a 24 × 10 cm/10 × 4 in terrine and pour over the court bouillon. Cook on HIGH for 2-3 minutes, until the liquid boils, then reduce the power to LOW and cook for 10-12 minutes, until the roll is just firm, carefully turning it over halfway through. Leave to cool, peel off the clingfilm, then slice and serve cold with tartare sauce.

# SEAFARERS' BAKED POTATOES

*These ever-popular baked potatoes are a marvellous way to use up leftover fish. If you like a crisp skin, cook the potatoes on Combination.*

SERVES 4

4 old potatoes, about 175 g/6 oz each
100 g/4 oz cooked white fish, flaked
75 g/3 oz canned red salmon, drained and flaked (optional)
2 tbsp chopped fresh parsley
100 g/4 oz soft cheese with garlic and herbs
2 tomatoes, skinned, deseeded and diced
salt and freshly ground black pepper
¼ tsp paprika

*1.* Scrub and dry the potatoes and prick them all over with a fork. Arrange them in a circle on a low rack and cook on COMBINATION 4 for 20-25 minutes. Alternatively, wrap each potato in a piece of kitchen paper and microwave on HIGH for 10-15 minutes, until soft, turning the potatoes over and rearranging them after 5 minutes.
*2.* Cut off the top third of each potato and reserve. Scoop out the flesh into a bowl. Keep about one-quarter for another use; there will not be enough room to put all the flesh back into the skin once you have mixed in the fish.
*3.* Mix the remainder with the fish, flaked salmon, if using, parsley, soft cheese and tomatoes. Season to taste with salt and pepper. Pile the mixture back into the skins, sprinkle with a pinch of paprika and top with the reserved 'lids'.
*4.* Heat on COMBINATION 4 for 5 minutes, or microwave on HIGH for 5 minutes, until very hot. Leave to stand for 5 minutes before serving.

# FISH PIE

*Fish pie need not be a pallid white affair. Add a touch of colour to the topping with carrots or swedes and use a mixture of smoked and fresh fish and plenty of flavouring to make this family dish one to look forward to.*

SERVES 4-6

450 g/1 lb cod or haddock fillets
225 g/8 oz smoked haddock or cod fillets
300 ml/½ pint milk
½ lemon, sliced
1 bay leaf
50 g/2 oz butter
25 g/1 oz plain flour
1 tbsp chopped fresh parsley
1 tsp anchovy essence (optional)
a pinch of cayenne pepper
salt and freshly ground black pepper
225 g/8 oz creamy mashed potato
225 g/8 oz carrots or swedes, cooked and mashed
25 g/1 oz mature Cheddar cheese, grated

*1.* Put the fish into a shallow dish with the milk, lemon slices and bay leaf. Cover and cook on HIGH for 6-8 minutes, until the fish flakes easily. Strain off and reserve the milk. Skin the fish and flake the flesh into a bowl, discarding any bones.
*2.* Put half the butter into a bowl and melt on HIGH for 45-60 seconds. Stir in the flour to make a roux, then gradually add the strained milk, stirring the sauce continuously. Cook on HIGH for 2 minutes, stirring halfway through.
*3.* Stir in the parsley, anchovy essence, if using, and the cayenne and season with salt and pepper if necessary – remember that both the smoked fish and anchovy essence are already salty.
*4.* Mix the sauce into the flaked fish, then transfer the mixture to a heatproof casserole or soufflé dish. Beat together the mashed potato, carrot or swede and the remaining butter until creamy, then spread the mixture evenly over the top of the fish. Fork up the surface and sprinkle with grated cheese. Cook on COMBINATION 5 for 15-20 minutes or microwave on HIGH for 5 minutes, then brown under a hot grill.

# KEDGEREE

*Cooked in the microwave, this old favourite comes out wonderfully creamy and tastes equally good hot or cold.*

SERVES 4-6

700 g/1 ½ lb smoked haddock on the bone
600 ml/1 pint milk
1 bay leaf
4 peppercorns
½ lemon, sliced
175 g/6 oz long grain rice
boiling water
1-2 pinches of curry powder
2 eggs
1-2 tbsp chopped fresh parsley
freshly ground black pepper
lemon juice
flat leaved parsley or sprigs of coriander, to garnish

*1.* Put the haddock into a shallow dish with the milk, bay leaf, peppercorns and lemon slices. Cover and cook on HIGH for 5 minutes, until the fish is tender. Leave to stand for 5 minutes, then strain off the cooking milk and reserve.
*2.* Put the rice into a casserole, make up the milk to 600 ml/1 pint with boiling water and pour it over the rice. Stir in curry powder to taste, cover and cook on HIGH for 7-8 minutes, until the rice is just tender. Leave to stand for 5 minutes.
*3.* Break the eggs into a ramekin, pierce the yolks with a cocktail stick, cover and cook on HIGH for 2-2½ minutes, until the whites are set. Leave to stand for 2 minutes until the yolks are just hard.
*4.* Remove the skin and bones from the haddock and flake the fish. Turn the eggs out of the ramekin, chop them roughly and fold them into the rice, together with the flaked fish and chopped parsley. If necessary, reheat on HIGH for 1-2 minutes. Season with a little pepper and a dash of lemon juice, if necessary, garnish with parsley or coriander and serve.

OVERLEAF *Left:* Kedgeree
*Right:* Mexican Fish Caramba (page 112)

# MEXICAN FISH CARAMBA

*This is the ideal dish for trying coley, which is always cheap, but often ignored because of its greyish flesh. The colourful vegetables will disguise the appearance of the fish and give it added flavour. Other white fish, such as cod, will do equally well. You can also use smoked mackerel instead of fresh; do not cook this before adding it to the vegetable mixture. If you are really pressed for time, use frozen mixed vegetables containing red pepper and sweetcorn.*

### SERVES 6

450 g/1 lb coley or cod fillets
225 g/8 oz mackerel fillets
freshly ground black pepper
50 g/2 oz butter
1 onion, sliced
2 cloves garlic, crushed
½ green pepper, cored, deseeded and finely diced
½ red pepper, cored, deseeded and finely diced
2 small courgettes, finely diced
100 g/4 oz sweetcorn kernels
2 tomatoes, skinned and chopped
juice of ½ fresh lime or 1 tbsp lemon juice
a pinch of cayenne pepper
a few drops of Tabasco sauce
salt
*Crumble topping*
50-75 g/2-3 oz tortilla chips, crushed
50 g/2 oz farmhouse Cheddar cheese, grated
a pinch of cayenne pepper

*1.* Arrange the fish in a shallow dish, grind over plenty of pepper, cover and cook on HIGH for 4 minutes. Leave to stand for 5 minutes, then remove the skin and flake the flesh.
*2.* Put the butter, onion and garlic in a round soufflé dish, cover and cook on HIGH for 3-4 minutes, until the onion is almost soft. Add the green and red peppers, stir well, cover and cook on HIGH for 2 minutes. Stir in the courgettes, cover and cook for another 3 minutes.
*3.* Mix in the sweetcorn, chopped tomatoes, lime or lemon juice and cayenne pepper, add Tabasco sauce to taste and season with salt and pepper.

Cover and cook on HIGH for 2 minutes, until the mixture is hot. Stir in the fish.
*4.* To make the topping, mix together the tortilla chips, Cheddar and cayenne pepper and sprinkle it over the fish mixture. Place under a preheated grill until the topping is crisp and brown.

# MILD FISH CURRY

*Introduce your family to the delights of ethnic foods with this delicately flavoured fish curry. Vary the quantity of spices in proportion to the adventurousness of your children. If they refuse even to try it, there will be all the more for the adults to enjoy!*

### SERVES 4

450 g/1 lb firm white fish fillets
1 tsp ground turmeric
1 tsp salt
½ tsp chilli powder
1 tsp ground cumin
1 tsp ground coriander
50 ml/2 fl oz boiling water
1 large potato, cut into 8 pieces
1 onion, coarsely chopped
3 tbsp sunflower oil
2 fresh green chillies, deseeded and thinly sliced
(optional – not recommended for young children!)
1-2 tbsp chopped fresh coriander, to garnish
poppadums, to serve

*1.* Cut the fish into 8 or 12 pieces. Mix together half the turmeric and half the salt and rub all over the fish. Set aside.
*2.* Put the remaining salt and spices in a small bowl and stir in the boiling water. Leave to infuse while you cook the vegetables.
*3.* Put the potato and onion in a casserole with the oil, cover and cook on HIGH for 5-7 minutes, until the potato is almost tender, stirring halfway through. Stir in the chillies, if using, then add the spice mixture and stir well to coat the potato pieces. Cook on HIGH for 2 minutes, stirring halfway through.

*4.* Pour in 200 ml/7 fl oz water and cook on HIGH for 2-3 minutes, until boiling. Arrange the pieces of fish on top of the vegetables, cover and cook on HIGH for 4-5 minutes, until the fish is tender.
*5.* Sprinkle with chopped coriander and serve with crisp poppadums.

# SMOKED MACKEREL FLAN

*This dish always seems popular with children. Why not give them a slice of cold flan to take to school for a packed lunch? The flan can be cooked in a combination oven, or bake the pastry case blind in a conventional oven and in the microwave.*

SERVES 4

225 g/8 oz shortcrust pastry
butter for greasing
100 g/4 oz smoked mackerel fillets
100 g/4 oz canned chopped tomatoes, drained
50 g/2 oz sweetcorn kernels
75 g/3 oz Cheddar cheese, grated
2 eggs
1 tsp paprika
salt and freshly ground black pepper
1 tomato, thinly sliced

*1.* Roll out the pastry on a floured surface and use to line a greased 20 cm/8 in flan dish. Place on the low rack and bake blind for 10 minutes on COMBINATION 2. alternatively, preheat a conventional oven to 220°C/425°F/Gas Mark 7 and bake the flan case blind for 12-15 minutes. Leave until cool.
*2.* Flake the mackerel into a bowl, discarding the skin and any bones. Add the tomatoes, corn and cheese, then spoon the mixture into the flan case. Beat the eggs with the paprika and a little salt and pepper and pour over the filling. Arrange the sliced tomato around the edge of the flan and cook on COMBINATION 2 for 10-12 minutes, until golden brown, or fill and microwave on MEDIUM for about 10 minutes, until the filling has set.

# FISH CRUMBLE

*Use any inexpensive white fish for this tasty crumble.*

SERVES 6

700 g/1 ½ lb white fish fillets
300 ml/½ pint milk
1 bay leaf
1 small onion, stuck with 2 cloves
1 blade of mace
25 g/1 oz butter
25 g/1 oz plain flour
salt and freshly ground pepper
3 hard-boiled eggs, chopped
100 g/4 oz cooked cockles
*Crumble topping*
50 g/2 oz butter, diced
50 g/2 oz plain flour
50 g/2 oz wholemeal flour
50 g/2 oz freshly grated Parmesan cheese

*1.* Put the fish into a dish with the milk, bay leaf, onion and mace. Cover and cook in HIGH for 6-8 minutes, until the fish flakes easily. Remove the fish from the dish, reserving the cooking liquid, and discard the skin and any bones and flake the flesh on to a plate.
*2.* Put the butter into a bowl and melt on HIGH for 45 seconds. Stir in the flour and cook on HIGH for 1 minute. Strain in the reserved milk from the fish, stirring continuously. Cook on HIGH for 3-4 minutes, or until thickened, stirring every minute. Season to taste with salt and pepper, then mix in the fish, eggs and cockles and put the mixture into a casserole or pie dish.
*3.* To make the crumble topping, rub the butter into the flours with your fingertips until the mixture clings together in large crumbs. Stir in the Parmesan cheese and sprinkle the crumble over the fish mixture.
*4.* Place the casserole on the low rack and cook on COMBINATION 3 for 20 minutes, until the topping is golden, or microwave on HIGH for 7-8 minutes, then brown under a preheated hot grill. Serve very hot.

# FISH CAKES

*Fish cakes need not be boring if you make them with really fresh fish and plenty of seasoning. The mistake many people make is to use ancient leftover fish and old mashed potato; this is a recipe for disaster! Fish cooks so quickly in the microwave that it is worth cooking it specially for the fish cakes; you can use any combination of fresh or smoked fish. To amuse the children, shape the cakes into fish or shell shapes before cooking. Cold fish cakes make good picnic or packed lunch fare.*

### SERVES 6

175-225 g/6-8 oz fresh brown breadcrumbs
450 g/1 lb cooked fish
450 g/1 lb freshly cooked potatoes
1 large egg
juice and grated zest of ½ lemon or 2 tsp anchovy essence
2 tbsp chopped fresh parsley
salt and freshly ground black pepper
100 ml/3 ½ fl oz sunflower oil

*1.* Spread the breadcrumbs in a baking dish and cook on HIGH for 2-3 minutes, until dry, then leave to cool. Put the crumbs in a plastic bag and crush with a rolling pin until they are as fine as you like them.
*2.* Flake the fish, discarding any skin and bones, and mash it with the potatoes, egg, lemon juice and zest or anchovy essence and parsley until smooth. Season to taste with salt and pepper.
*3.* Divide the mixture into 12 portions and shape each into a flat round cake, fish or other shapes. Press both sides into the breadcrumbs to coat them evenly.
*4.* Heat a browning dish on HIGH for 5-8 minutes, or according to the manufacturer's instructions. Add half the oil and heat on HIGH for 1 minute.
*5.* Add half the fish cakes and cook on HIGH for 2 minutes, until the underside of each is crisp and browned. Turn them over with a fish slice and

cook on HIGH for about 3 minutes, until browned on both sides. Drain on kitchen paper while you cook the rest of the fish cakes.
*6.* Wipe out the browning dish with kitchen paper, taking care not to burn yourself, then heat it on HIGH for another 3-4 minutes. Add the remaining oil, heat on HIGH for 1 minute, then cook the fish cakes as before. Drain them and serve hot or cold.

# ARBROATH SMOKIES WITH BACON

*Arbroath smokies are hot-smoked haddock from Scotland. They have a more delicate flavour and a softer texture than most smoked haddock and are a favourite Scottish supper or breakfast dish. They are not usually split open, so ask the fishmonger to do this for you. If you cannot find smokies, use whole finnan haddie.*

### SERVES 2

2 Arbroath smokies, split, or 2 finnan haddie
25 g/1 oz butter
4 rashers unsmoked back bacon
freshly ground black pepper
fresh herbs, to garnish

*1.* Lay the smokies in a shallow dish, dot with butter, cover and cook on HIGH for 6-8 minutes, rearranging the fish halfway through. Leave to stand for 5 minutes.
*2.* Meanwhile, remove the bacon rinds and lay the rashers on a roasting rack or a double thickness of kitchen paper. Cover with 2 more layers of paper and cook for 3½-4½ minutes, depending how crisp you like your bacon.
*3.* Put the smokies on warmed plates, pour over the cooking butter and grind over some pepper. Top each smokie with 2 rashers of bacon, garnish with fresh herbs and serve at once.

Arbroath Smokies with Bacon

# SPAGHETTI AL CARTOCCIO

*I have included this recipe for spaghetti in a paper bag as a family dish, because my own family thinks it is the ultimate in pasta dishes. In fact, the heavenly smell as you cut open the bag makes this a meal to grace any occasion. Vary the shellfish to suit your taste and pocket.*

SERVES 4

225-350 g/8-12 oz spaghetti
salt
1 tbsp olive oil
1 dried red chilli, chopped (optional)
2-4 cloves garlic, finely chopped (the more you use, the more pungent the smell will be when you open the bag)
175g/6 oz squid, cleaned and cut into thin rings
450 g/1 lb small clams, scrubbed
450 g/1 lb mussels, scrubbed and debearded
200 g/7 oz can chopped tomatoes
1 tbsp finely chopped fresh parsley
freshly ground black pepper

*1.* Cook the spaghetti conventionally in plenty of boiling salted water until barely *al dente.* Meanwhile, prepare the seafood sauce.
*2.* Put the oil into a large shallow dish and heat on HIGH for 1 minute. Stir in the chilli, if using, the garlic and squid rings. Cover and cook on HIGH for 3 minutes, until the squid is opaque.
*3.* Lift the squid out of the dish with a slotted spoon and transfer it to a large bowl. Put the clams into the oil in the dish and cook on HIGH for 4 minutes, stirring halfway through. Discard any clams which have not opened, remove most of the others from their shells (I like to keep a few in the shell; they look pretty in the sauce) and add them to the squid.
*4.* Put the mussels into the hot oil and cook on HIGH for 4-5 minutes, shaking the dish every 2 minutes. Discard any mussels which have not opened.
*5.* Remove the cooked mussels from their shells and stir them into the oil in the dish. Add the clams, squid, tomatoes and parsley and season

to taste with salt and plenty of pepper.
*6.* Make a double thickness of greaseproof paper about 40 × 50 cm/16 × 20 in and lay it in a deep platter. Drain the spaghetti and stir it into the sauce. Pile the spaghetti and sauce into the middle of the greaseproof paper. Pull up the longer edges of the paper and fold over twice. Twist the ends to make a sealed bag.
*7.* Cook the bag of spaghetti on HIGH for 3 minutes, until very hot, then open up the bag and let the glorious aroma waft out. Serve at once.

# FISH COBBLER

*Any white fish can be used in this delicious pie with its savoury scone topping, which can be cooked either in a combination or conventional oven. For a special treat, add a few prawns or other shellfish.*

SERVES 4-6

700 g/1 ½ lb haddock or cod fillets, skinned
50 g/2 oz butter
1 onion, sliced
2 cloves garlic, crushed
2 celery stalks, sliced
1 leek, sliced
400 g/14 oz can chopped tomatoes
1 tbsp tomato purée
2 tbsp concentrated Fish stock (see p. 20)
bouquet garni
salt and freshly ground black pepper
*Scone topping*
200 g/7 oz self-raising flour
a pinch of salt
50 g/2 oz butter
½ tsp paprika
½ tsp dried mixed herbs
150 ml/5 fl oz milk, plus 1 tsp to glaze

*1.* Cut the fish into bite-sized chunks and set aside.
*2.* In a casserole, heat the butter on HIGH for 2 minutes, until melted. Add the onion, garlic, celery and leek, cover and cook on HIGH for 5 minutes, until soft.

*3.* Stir in the tomatoes, purée, stock and bouquet garni and season to taste. Cook on HIGH for 3 minutes, then stir in the fish, cover and cook on HIGH for 6 minutes. Remove the bouquet garni.

*4.* To make the scone topping, sift the flour and salt into a bowl and rub in the butter until the mixture resembles fine breadcrumbs. Add the paprika and herbs and enough of the milk to make a soft dough. Knead lightly on a floured surface, then roll out to about 2 cm/¾ in thick. Cut into rounds with a 5 cm/2 in pastry cutter and arrange the rounds over the fish in the casserole, overlapping them slightly.

*5.* Brush lightly with milk, place on the low rack and cook on COMBINATION 2 for 10-12 minutes, until the topping is risen and golden, or bake in a preheated conventional oven at 220°C/425°F/Gas Mark 7 for 8-10 minutes.

# QUICK SEAFOOD LASAGNE

*Rustle up this filling lasagne in less than half an hour and vary the shellfish as you like (defrost frozen shellfish first). You can also add any cooked white fish to give more variety.*

SERVES 4-6

8 sheets of lasagne
boiling water
1 tsp salt
200 g/7 oz canned tuna, drained and flaked
100 g/4 oz cooked cockles
100 g/4 oz cooked peeled prawns
175 g/6 oz cooked white crabmeat or white fish, flaked
225 g/8 oz cooked mussels
50 g/2 oz Gruyère or Cheddar cheese, grated
*Sauce*
50 g/2 oz butter
50 g/2 oz plain flour
¼ tsp mustard powder
salt and freshly ground black pepper
300 ml/½ pint milk
300 ml/½ pint white wine or Fish stock (see p. 20)

*1.* Cook the lasagne conventionally, or put it in a large rectangular dish, cover with boiling water, add 1 tsp salt and cook on HIGH for 7-9 minutes, until *al dente*. Drain and dry on kitchen paper.

*2.* Meanwhile, mix together all the fish and shellfish in a bowl and put to one side.

*3.* To make the sauce, melt the butter in a bowl on HIGH for 1-2 minutes. Stir in the flour and mustard powder and cook on HIGH for 1 minute to make a roux. Stir well and season to taste with salt and freshly ground pepper.

*4.* Pour the milk and wine or fish stock into a jug and heat on HIGH for 2 minutes. Gradually pour the liquid into the roux, stirring continuously until smooth. Cook on HIGH for 3 minutes, until the sauce is thick and smooth, stirring every minute.

*5.* To assemble the lasagne, layer it into the rectangular dish, starting with a layer of lasagne, then one of seafood, then sauce, finishing with a thick layer of sauce. Sprinkle over the cheese.

*6.* Place the dish on the low rack and cook on COMBINATION 2 for 20 minutes, or microwave on HIGH for 10-12 minutes, until the lasagne is hot and bubbling. Leave to stand for 5 minutes before serving.

One of the nicest meals for a summer's day is an attractively presented fish salad. Microwaving fish keeps in all the moisture so that it remains deliciously juicy and tender when cold. A refreshing chilled fish salad will tempt you to eat even on a hot day when you are not hungry.

All the cold salads can be prepared several hours in advance. Chill the fish once it is cooked, but take it out of the fridge about 30 minutes before serving to allow the flavour to come through.

Garnish the salads with bright fresh herbs or even edible flowers; they are summer dishes, so make the most of what the season has to offer.

Thanks to modern methods of transportation, many shellfish are now available even in those months without an 'r' in them, so you should be able to make the salads with fresh shellfish. If you cannot find scallops in September, for example, substitute something else; these salads must be made with fresh shellfish – frozen will not do, but any firm white fish, like monkfish or perhaps cod can be used instead. Be adventurous and experiment with what is in season.

# SALADS

CHAPTER 6

# HUSS WITH TUNA MAYONNAISE

*Huss (otherwise known as rock salmon) has a rather bad name, probably because it formerly delighted in the unattractive alias of dogfish, but in fact the flavour is delicious. Do try this unusual salad, which makes a most delicious lunch dish. If you can find them, decorate the salad with nasturtium flowers (some supermarkets sell them in packets on the salad counter); they add a glorious splash of colour and a pleasant peppery taste.*

SERVES 4

450 g/1 lb huss
1 small onion
1 bay leaf
salt
1 lettuce heart, chopped
100 g/4 oz can tuna in oil, drained
4 anchovy fillets
1 tbsp capers
juice of ½ lemon
150 ml/5 fl oz Mayonnaise (see p. 25)
¼ cucumber, thinly sliced, to serve
*Garnish*
anchovy fillets
lemon slices
capers

*1.* Put the fish into a shallow dish with the onion, bay leaf, a large pinch of salt and 300 ml/½ pint water. Cover and cook on HIGH for 4-5 minutes, until the fish is tender.

*2.* Leave to cool in the cooking liquid, then lift out the fish and remove the backbone and any small bones, keeping the pieces of fish as large as possible. Arrange on a bed of chopped lettuce and chill in the fridge.

*3.* To make the tuna mayonnaise, purée the tuna, anchovies and capers with the lemon juice in a blender or food processor until very smooth, then blend in the mayonnaise. Taste and season as necessary.

*4.* Pour the tuna mayonnaise over the fish, then surround with a circle of overlapping cucumber slices and serve, garnished with a lattice of anchovy fillets, lemon slices and capers.

# PIQUANT PRAWN SALAD

*Serve the prawns on a bed of mixed green salad leaves dressed with a sesame oil vinaigrette. They also make a very good hot starter or lunch dish, served with a little rice. Use more than one fresh chilli if you can bear it.*

SERVES 4

450 g/1 lb cooked peeled prawns
3 tbsp Chinese rice wine or dry sherry
1 clove garlic, crushed
1 cm/½ in ginger root, peeled and crushed or very finely chopped
1 fresh red or green chilli, deseeded and very finely sliced
2 spring onions, very finely sliced
salt
1 tbsp sesame seeds

*1.* Put the prawns, rice wine or sherry, garlic, ginger and chilli into a large bowl, stir well, then cover and cook on HIGH for 3 minutes.

*2.* Stir in the spring onions and season with salt. Leave to cool, then chill.

*3.* Spread the sesame seeds in a shallow dish and cook on HIGH for 1-2 minutes, until toasted. Sprinkle them over the chilled prawns at the last moment.

# WARM MONKFISH AND CHICKEN LIVER SALAD

*Normally, I am not enthusiastic about cooking fish and meat together, but here the combination of firm, juicy monkfish and melting chicken livers is irresistible. The slightly bitter salad offsets the richness of the dish. Scallops make a heavenly alternative to the monkfish.*

SERVES 4

4 fresh chicken livers
350 g/12 oz monkfish fillet, skinned
2 tbsp olive oil
50 g/2 oz cornsalad
50 g/2 oz curly endive
50 g/2 oz radicchio
25 g/1 oz rocket or nasturtium leaves
*Dressing*
1 tbsp sherry vinegar
2-3 tbsp walnut or olive oil
salt and freshly ground black pepper

*1.* Clean and halve the chicken livers, carefully trimming off the bitter greenish gall. Pierce the livers with the point of a knife to prevent them from bursting during cooking. Cut the monkfish into bite-sized chunks.
*2.* Heat a browning dish on HIGH for 5-8 minutes, or according to the manufacturer's instructions. Pour in the olive oil and immediately stir in the chicken livers and monkfish.
*3.* Cover and cook on HIGH for 1 minute, then turn over the livers and fish and cook on HIGH for another 1-2 minutes, stirring halfway through. The livers should be very pink and the monkfish barely cooked. Leave them to stand while you prepare the salad.
*4.* Wash and dry all the salad leaves and place in a bowl. Add the sherry vinegar, oil and salt and pepper to taste and toss well. Arrange the salad decoratively on individual plates, then spoon on the chicken livers and monkfish with their cooking juices. Serve at once.

# HAKE SALAD

*For some reason, hake has never been a popular fish in Britain, although its flaky texture and delicate flavour make it suitable for all kinds of dishes. Try it in this substantial salad.*

SERVES 4

450 g/1 lb hake
150 ml/5 fl oz Court bouillon (see p. 20) or dry white wine
1 onion, finely sliced
1 bay leaf
450 g/1 lb tiny new potatoes, cooked
½ red pepper, deseeded and diced
100 g/4 oz petits pois or mange-tout, cooked
2 spring onions, finely chopped
½ cucumber, unpeeled and diced
1-2 tbsp capers
salt and freshly ground black pepper
4 lollo rosso lettuce or radicchio leaves, to serve
*Dressing*
150 ml/5 fl oz Greek-style yogurt
2 tbsp olive oil
juice of ½ lemon
1 tbsp chopped fresh chervil
2 tbsp finely snipped fresh chives

*1.* Put the hake into a dish with the court bouillon or wine, sliced onion and bay leaf. Cover and cook on HIGH for 5 minutes.
*2.* Leave to stand for 5 minutes, then remove the skin and bones (hake bones are very easy to remove). Chill the fish and cut into chunks.
*3.* If any potatoes are too large, halve them, then place in a bowl with the red pepper, peas, spring onions, cucumber and capers. Season to taste with salt and pepper.
*4.* Mix together all the dressing ingredients, season with salt and pepper, then pour over the salad and mix carefully and thoroughly. Serve the salad on a red lettuce leaf on individual plates.

# INSALATA DI MARE

*This Italian seafood salad normally contains a high proportion of squid, but I prefer to include a good selection of other seafood. You can vary the ingredients as you wish.*

### SERVES 6

450 g/1 lb mussels, scrubbed and debearded
450 g/1 lb small clams, scrubbed
100 ml/3 ½ fl oz dry vermouth
225 g/8 oz squid, cleaned
2 tbsp olive oil
2 cloves garlic, finely chopped
350 g/12 oz hake or any firm white fish
225 g/8 oz cooked unpeeled prawns
*Dressing*
1 tbsp lemon juice
2 tbsp white wine vinegar
½ tsp Dijon mustard
sea salt and coarsely ground black pepper
120 ml/4 fl oz olive oil
*To serve*
1 head of chicory, separated into leaves
6 radicchio leaves
3 tbsp finely chopped fresh chervil

*1.* Put the mussels and clams into a large dish with the vermouth and cook on HIGH for 4-6 minutes, shaking the dish every 2 minutes. Discard any unopened mussels and clams.
*2.* Cut the squid into thin rings. If they are very small, cut the tentacles into 1-cm/½-in lengths and leave the bodies whole.
*3.* Heat the oil in a large dish on HIGH for 1 minute, add the garlic, hake and squid, cover and cook on HIGH for 4-5 minutes, stirring halfway through. Strain off and reserve the oil.
*4.* Strain the cooking liquid from the mussels and clams into a bowl and cook on HIGH for 8-10 minutes until reduced by half. Remove half the mussels and clams from their shells and mix both shelled and unshelled molluscs with the squid and hake. Stir in the prawns.
*5.* To make the dressing, mix together the lemon juice, vinegar and mustard and season to taste. Add the olive oil, whisk vigorously, then whisk in the reserved vermouth and the cooking oil and pour over the seafood salad. Chill lightly.
*6.* Arrange the seafood salad, chicory and radicchio attractively on a serving platter, sprinkle with chopped chervil and serve.

# SCALLOP AND MANGE-TOUT SALAD

*Crunchy mange-tout combine well with the sweet scallops in this refreshing salad. If you prepare it in advance, take it out of the fridge half an hour before serving, or the flavours will not come through. If you use balsamic vinegar use it sparingly as it is very strong.*

### SERVES 4

2 handfuls of frisée, batavia or attractive pale lettuce
100 g/4 oz mange-tout, topped and tailed
a pinch of caster sugar
1 tbsp hazelnut oil
1 tbsp butter
12-16 shelled queen scallops
2 spring onions, very finely sliced
*Dressing*
2 tsp sherry vinegar or 1 tsp balsamic vinegar
2 tbsp hazelnut oil
salt and freshly ground black pepper

*1.* Wash, dry and tear the salad leaves. Whisk the dressing ingredients together and toss the leaves in the dressing. Arrange it on 4 serving plates.
*2.* Put the mange-tout into a dish with 2 tbsp water and the sugar, cover and cook on HIGH for 1½-2 minutes; they should still be very crunchy. Refresh in cold water, drain and set aside.
*3.* Heat the oil and butter in a shallow dish on HIGH for 1 minute, then add the scallops. Cover and cook on HIGH for 1 minute, turning them over halfway through.
*4.* Stir in the spring onions and mange-tout and spoon the mixture over the prepared salad.

*Top:* Insalata di Mare
*Bottom:* Scallop and Mange-tout Salad

# SCAMPI AND AVOCADO SALAD

*If your avocados are slightly under-ripe, soften them for 1 minute each on HIGH and leave to cool before serving. The texture will improve greatly.*

SERVES 4-6

2 tbsp olive oil
450 g/1 lb fresh scampi tails, peeled
50 g/2 oz frisée or batavia lettuce
50 g/2 oz cornsalad
25 g/1 oz watercress leaves
2 blood oranges or small navel oranges
2 avocados
lemon juice
*Dressing*
2 tbsp lemon juice
2 tbsp orange juice
2 tbsp sunflower oil
1 tbsp olive oil
1 tbsp chopped fresh chervil
1 tbsp chopped fresh tarragon
salt and freshly ground black pepper

*1.* Put the oil into a large dish and heat on HIGH for 1 minute. Stir in the scampi and cook for 2-3 minutes, until opaque, stirring halfway through. Pour off the oil and keep it for the dressing.
*2.* Wash and carefully dry all the salad leaves. Tear the lettuce into small pieces and put it into a bowl with the cornsalad and watercress.
*3.* Peel the oranges, removing all the pith, and cut out the segments between the membranes. Use the juice from the core for the dressing.
*4.* Slice the avocados and dip the slices briefly in lemon juice to prevent discoloration.
*5.* Put all the ingredients for the dressing in a screw top jar, seasoning to taste with salt and pepper. Add the reserved oil and orange juice and shake vigorously. Pour half the dressing over the salad leaves and toss well.
*6.* Divide the salad leaves between individual plates and arrange the sliced avocado and orange segments around the edge. Top the salad with the lightly cooked scampi and drizzle over the remaining dressing. Serve immediately.

# MUSSEL SALAD

*Serve this light salad either cold or just warm, on a bed of contrasting salad leaves (frisée, radicchio and cornsalad), or by itself as a starter.*

SERVES 4-6

2 kg/4 ½ lb mussels, scrubbed and debearded
2 shallots or ½ Spanish onion, chopped
1 clove garlic, finely chopped
2 sprigs thyme
2 sprigs parsley
1 bay leaf
4 coriander seeds, lightly crushed
150 ml/5 fl oz dry white wine
4 tbsp chopped fresh coriander, to garnish
*Dressing*
2 tbsp red wine vinegar
3 tbsp olive oil
salt and freshly ground black pepper

*1.* Put half the mussels into a large bowl with the shallots or onion, garlic, herbs, coriander seeds and wine. Cover and cook on HIGH for 5 minutes, stirring halfway through.
*2.* Discard any cooked mussels which have not opened and, using a slotted spoon, transfer the rest to another bowl. Keep the cooking liquid. Cook the remaining mussels in the same way, using the reserved cooking liquid. When cool, remove the mussels from their shells.
*3.* To make the dressing, whisk together ½ tbsp of the strained cooking liquid, the wine vinegar, olive oil and salt and pepper to taste.
*4.* Toss the mussels in the dressing, leave to cool, then drain off any excess dressing and serve the mussels in an attractive dish, sprinkled with chopped coriander.

# INDEX